Color Tab Index

 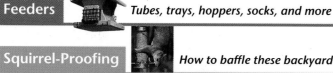

Stokes Field Guides

Stokes Field Guide to Birds: Eastern Region

Stokes Field Guide to Birds: Western Region

Stokes Field Guide to Bird Songs: Eastern Region (CD/cassette)

Stokes Field Guide to Bird Songs: Western Region (CD/cassette)

Stokes Beginner's Guides

Stokes Beginner's Guide to Bats

Stokes Beginner's Guide to Birds: Eastern Region

Stokes Beginner's Guide to Birds: Western Region

Stokes Beginner's Guide to Butterflies

Stokes Beginner's Guide to Dragonflies

Stokes Beginner's Guide to Shorebirds

Stokes Backyard Nature Books

Stokes Bird Feeder Book

Stokes Bird Gardening Book

Stokes Birdhouse Book

Stokes Bluebird Book

Stokes Butterfly Book

Stokes Hummingbird Book

Stokes Oriole Book

Stokes Purple Martin Book

Stokes Wildflower Book: East of the Rockies

Stokes Wildflower Book: From the Rockies West

Stokes Nature Guides

Stokes Guide to Amphibians and Reptiles

Stokes Guide to Animal Tracking and Behavior

Stokes Guide to Bird Behavior, Volume 1

Stokes Guide to Bird Behavior, Volume 2

Stokes Guide to Bird Behavior, Volume 3

Stokes Guide to Enjoying Wildflowers

Stokes Guide to Nature in Winter

Stokes Guide to Observing Insect Lives

Other Stokes Books

The Natural History of Wild Shrubs and Vines

STOKES
Beginner's Guide
to Bird Feeding

Donald and Lillian Stokes   MAPS BY **Thomas Young**

Little, Brown and Company
New York   Boston   London

Little, Brown and Company
Hachette Book Group
1290 Avenue of the Americas, New York, NY 10104
littlebrown.com

First Edition

Little, Brown and Company is a division of
Hachette Book Group, Inc. The Little, Brown
name and logo are trademarks of Hachette Book
Group, Inc.

The publisher is not responsible for websites (or
their content) that are not owned by the publisher.

ISBN 978-0-316-81659-5
Library of Congress Control Number 2002090672

13

IM

Manufactured in China

Photo Credits

A letter or letters following a page number refer
to the position of the picture on the page (T=top;
B=bottom; L=left; R=right).

Aspects, Inc.: 9, 32L, 40, 44.
Lindsey Brown: 10, 14L, 31L, 77, 94, 95.
Mike Danzenbaker: 71, 87.
Droll Yankees, Inc.: 42.
Bruce Flaig: 3, 6.
Kevin Karlson: 43R, 93, 118R.
Anthony Mercieca: 67, 73, 74, 75, 88, 92, 99, 101R,
    103, 118L.
Clair Postmus: 16, 109L, 124R.
Brian Small: 70, 79, 81, 84, 89, 90, 97, 104, 112R,
    115R, 117, 121, 122, 123L, 123TR, 124L.
Tom Vezo: 17R, 41R, 43L, 62, 64, 72, 76, 78, 80, 82,
    85, 86, 91, 98, 100L, 100R, 101L, 102T, 102B,
    105, 106, 107, 108, 109R, 110, 111, 112L, 113L,
    114, 115L, 116, 119, 120, 123BR, 125.

All other photographs are by Lillian Stokes.

Contents

Introduction

Feeding wild birds is one of the most enjoyable, absorbing, and rewarding lifetime hobbies. Not only do you get to see birds up close, which is a real thrill, but you also have the satisfaction

Black-capped Chickadee

of feeding and helping out a wild animal. Feeding and attracting birds is part of a large trend toward turning our backyards into wildlife sanctuaries, peaceful and stress-reducing places that nurture the birds and are havens for us. Humans have probably been feeding birds in some way ever since our early ancestry, for birds are curious and always looking for food.

BIRD FEEDING AS A HOBBY

Various studies have been done on how many Americans feed birds in their own backyards. Most seem to suggest that about 65 million people take part. This includes all levels of involvement with the hobby, from people who only put out a little seed

every once in a while to those who have ten or more feeders and go through over 100 pounds of seed a week.

There are many ways to participate in bird feeding, and whether you live in urban or rural areas, there are lots of birds to attract. You can feed birds just one kind of seed, or you can offer many types of seed in a wide variety of feeders, as well as offering suet, nuts, fruit, and sugar water. If you are like most people, you will find bird feeding a fun and absorbing hobby, and you will soon get caught up in wanting to attract more species of birds, in greater numbers, more of the time.

WHEN TO FEED BIRDS

Determining when to feed birds is easy. Feed them all year. It will increase your enjoyment, and birds can use our help

A backyard habitat with diversity

insects are only just beginning to fill the air, so birds — both year-round residents and returning migrants — especially need feeder foods in spring. In summer, birds are raising young, and this takes a lot of effort. Offering food at this time helps parents feed themselves easily so they can spend more time looking for food to feed their young. Later, the parents may bring their young to the feeder, where the young eventually learn to feed themselves.

WHY FEED BIRDS?

There are so many good reasons to feed wild birds. One is that with every new building and road, we humans are taking away habitat that produces seeds, berries, and insects that the birds need to survive. Attracting birds by providing sources of food and bird-friendly

in every month. Each season has its challenges for the birds, and the seed and other foods that we can offer help them throughout their lives. In fall, many birds are on migration and need extra food to help fuel them on their long journeys. In winter, it is colder and the birds that don't migrate need more calories to keep them warm. In spring, most of the food in the wild, such as all of the seeds and berries, has been eaten during the winter, and new

Male American Goldfinches on a feeder with hulled sunflower chips

habitat can help offset in small measure some of these losses of habitats and the foods they produce.

Feeding the birds is extremely educational. It is a great introduction to the natural world for all ages. It brings birds up close so they can be seen in all their beauty; it teaches what birds like to eat, how they feed, and what they need for survival; and it's an easy way to begin learning to identify birds. It can be a wonderful family activity, and a way for parents or grandparents to introduce children to nature and the world of birds.

Bird feeding is also very relaxing and inspirational. It brings joy to all ages, keeps older people in touch with nature and life, and gives young people an awareness of the greater natural world of which they are a part. Watching birds outside a home or office window can do wonders to reduce stress and is a boon to a healthier outlook on life.

And finally, feeding the birds can give you a strong sense of well-being, because you are doing something positive for the world. It is almost magical when you put out feeders and the birds actually come; you have met their needs and they are responding. In addition to setting up feeders, creating good varied habitats in our own backyards provides the birds with essential natural sources of food and nesting places. Attracting birds is a thrilling interaction with the natural world and a way to exercise the best of our nurturing instincts as humans for the life around us. It can also inspire us to become more involved with wildlife conservation on a larger scale.

We hope this introduction to the hobby of bird feeding will start you out on a lifelong activity that enriches your world and benefits the lives of birds.

How to Use This Guide

This book is designed for easy use. The handy color tab index at the front of the book will lead you quickly to the topic you're interested in. If you have never fed birds before, turn first to the section called Five Steps to Bird-Feeding Success. People who are already feeding birds can browse through the Seeds and Other Foods and Feeders chapters to learn about new options. Everybody should read the Squirrel-Proofing section, not only for themselves, but also to help others who may complain about squirrels; most squirrel problems *can* be solved. The Identification Pages will help you identify the birds that come to your feeders and also tell you how to go about attracting certain species that you may especially want. If you have problems attracting birds, have birds you do not want at your feeders, or experience other problems in relation to feeding birds, see Solving Feeder Problems. This explains how to deal with the most common problems people have with their feeders.

FIVE STEPS TO BIRD-FEEDING SUCCESS

If you are an absolute beginner, check out this chapter first. Here you will learn what to put out first to attract birds and how to go about it. The chapter also offers suggestions on how to expand the foods you offer and the feeders you use to attract a greater number and variety of birds.

Male Downy Woodpecker and male Northern Cardinal on tubular feeder filled with black oil sunflower seed

SEEDS AND OTHER FOODS

This handy section shows you color pictures of all the different foods you can offer birds. For each food there is a detailed description of where it comes from, how to recognize it, what types of feeders to place it in, and the most common birds that it attracts.

Female Northern Cardinal

FEEDERS

This chapter is an introduction to the basic types of feeders that can be used at your feeding station. It explains their structure, uses, advantages, and limitations, and tells you the key features to look for when buying one. It also discusses what to consider in setting up a feeding station and how to care for your feeders.

SQUIRREL-PROOFING

Whenever people discuss bird feeding, one of the first topics of conversation is squirrels. Whether you love them or hate them, squirrels show up at feeders and have to be dealt with. This chapter shows you the most successful ways to keep squirrels off your feeders, and then continues on with ways to feed and entertain squirrels (and yourself!) if you so desire.

SOLVING FEEDER PROBLEMS

Over the 25 years that we have been teaching people about nature, birds, and attracting wildlife, we have answered thousands of questions on feeding birds. The great majority of these fall into just a few categories: squirrels and how to deal with them, figuring out why there are no birds at your feeders, selective feeding (getting some species but excluding others), and types of seed and feeders. In this section, we answer the questions you are most likely to have.

IDENTIFICATION PAGES

This section contains information on the identification and lives of the 57 most common feeder birds. Each species account starts with the bird's name in large letters, followed by its scientific name in smaller italic letters. Then the length of the bird is given, measured from the tip of its bill to the tip of its tail. Each account also includes the following:

Identification — This section focuses on the main features of the bird that distinguish it from other species. There is a color photograph of each species; when male and female of a species differ substantially in appearance, both are shown. The identification section also describes the main sounds that you may hear the bird make.

Feeding — Here you will find information on the feeder foods preferred by each bird and also the kind of feeder that works best for that bird.

Landscaping — Every bird has habitat requirements and preferences, both for feeding and nesting. In this section, we indicate steps you can take to make your yard or feeder setup more inviting.

Breeding — Here you will learn about the birds' nesting habits as well as details of the nesting cycle, including average number and color of eggs; the number of days spent *incubating* the eggs (I); the time from when the eggs hatch until the young can first fly, a moment called *fledging* (F); and the number of times a year an individual bird is likely to go through a complete nesting cycle, or *brood* (B).

Range Map — This map gives you a good idea of whether a bird is likely to be found in your area during a particular season. The blue portion shows where the bird lives in winter, the yellow is the summer range, and the green portion shows where these summer and winter ranges overlap and thus where the bird can be found all year.

Fun Facts — These are interesting or unusual facts about the birds that we hope will spur your curiosity to learn more.

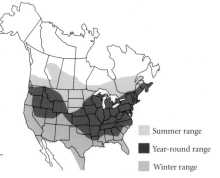

Summer range

Year-round range

Winter range

Five Steps to Bird-Feeding Success

KEYS TO SUCCESS

The best way to attract birds is to provide food, water, shelter, and nesting places. Food and water are easy to provide. But with the bewildering number of feeders and seed mixes available,

THE BASIC FEEDER SETUP

Five Easy Steps

1. Sunflower seed in a tube or hopper feeder
2. Thistle (Nyjer) seed in a tubular feeder
3. Mixed seed in a hopper or tray feeder
4. Suet
5. Water

A successful feeder setup offering (l.–r.) hulled sunflower seed in a tube feeder, suet in a suet cage, mixed seed in a hopper feeder, and thistle (Nyjer) in a tube feeder. A baffle on the pole beneath the feeders will keep squirrels off

how can you be sure that you have selected the right ones? This chapter contains the five steps that our years of experience have shown will create a successful bird-feeding station and will attract the most birds.

Depending on your interest and experience, you may want to start with just one or two of the steps. In this case, begin with step one, then move on to step two, and so forth. But remember, if you want more birds, you will eventually want to have all five steps represented in your feeding station. This chapter is just a summary; for complete information on choosing seeds and feeders and setting up and maintaining feeders, see the chapters that follow.

1. Sunflower seed in a tube or hopper feeder

Sunflower seed is the number-one choice of seeds among the widest variety of birds. The seed can be offered either hulled or with the hulls on. Place it in a tubular feeder or a hopper feeder and hang it from a pole with a hook at the top.

Use a baffle on the pole to keep squirrels off (see pages 50–51 for pictures of baffles).

2. Thistle (Nyjer) seed in a tubular feeder

Thistle seed (also called Nyjer seed) is a top choice of finches, such as goldfinches, and is an important staple of any good feeding station. Thistle is often combined with other small seeds into a "finch mix," a more economical

Tubular feeder with hulled sunflower seed

way to feed finches, since straight thistle is expensive. Place the thistle or finch mix in a tubular feeder especially designed with small holes for tiny seeds. These are sometimes referred to as finch feeders. Hang it off a pole along with your sunflower feeder.

3. Mixed seed in a hopper or tray feeder

Mixed seed can attract a variety of birds and should be placed in a tray or hopper feeder. Trays and hopper feeders with their wide ledges both enable birds that usually feed on the ground to come to feeders. This hopper or tray feeder can be hung from a pole like the tubular feeders, or the tray feeder can be placed on the ground (see page 36 for photos of tray feeders).

Use a baffle on the pole to keep squirrels off.

Goldfinch at thistle feeder; note the small hole allowing access to the tiny seeds

A hopper feeder (also called ranch feeder) with mixed seed

4. Suet

Suet is a high-fat food that offers birds a concentrated source of energy (see pages 26–27 for more about suet). Commercial suet cakes especially for birds are widely available, and they fit into handy wire mesh holders. These attract some birds that do not as

Birdbath

Suet cake in a hanging basket

readily come to seed, such as woodpeckers, as well as many seed-eating birds. Suet in a holder can also be hung from a pole, or the feeder can be attached to a tree trunk.

5. Water

All birds need water for bathing and drinking. Be sure to put out a small birdbath near your feeders. This will not only help your feeder birds but will also attract other species that normally would not be attracted by seed or suet.

If you do these five things, you will have the best chances of attracting birds and having a successful feeder setup.

MORE ADVANCED FEEDER SETUPS

Once you have accomplished the basic setup, you may soon be ready to expand the foods you offer. Take a look at the other chapters in this book to familiarize yourself with the options, and think about what kinds of birds you want to attract. Here are some specific steps you can take:

◆ Try new foods, such as different seed mixes, fruits, jelly, and nuts. See Seeds and Other Foods, page 17, for a full range of ideas.
◆ Try additional feeders that are slightly different from the ones you are using and see how they work in your yard. See Feeders, page 31.
◆ Try offering sugar water for hummingbirds and orioles. See page 27.

Male Scarlet Tanager at an orange half

◆ Add plantings to your yard that birds will like, such as berry-producing trees and shrubs, and flowers that offer nectar. To learn more about this, check out some of the publications and organizations in Resources, page 126.

Seeds, feeders, mounting poles, and other accessories can be purchased from the many retailers across the country who sell bird-feeding supplies.

Seeds and Other Foods

BLACK OIL SUNFLOWER SEED

Black oil sunflower is a small seed that is all black. It is the number-one choice of the majority of birds that visit feeders. This is because it has a high oil content, which provides the birds with lots of energy, and a thin shell that is easy for the birds to open. Black oil sunflower is the key to a successful bird-feeding program, so try to have at least one feeder dedicated to it.

Black oil sunflower is also a component of many mixed seeds. Since it is a more expensive seed than other common components of mixed seed — such as corn, milo, or millet — seed mixes are usually graded in quality and expense by how much black oil sunflower they contain. Expensive mixes have a higher percentage of black oil; cheaper mixes have a smaller percentage. Generally more birds will be attracted to the mixes with the higher percentage of black oil sunflower.

How to offer: It is best offered in hanging tube feeders, hopper feeders, or

Black oil sunflower seed

Male Northern Cardinal; cardinals are among the many birds attracted by sunflower seed

platform feeders mounted above the ground.

Birds attracted: Appeals to many species, especially birds that feed above ground level, including chickadees, titmice, nuthatches, goldfinches and other finches, cardinals, grosbeaks, and jays.

STRIPED SUNFLOWER SEED

Striped sunflower is a large black-and-white-striped seed. Since it has a somewhat lower fat content and harder shell than black oil sunflower seed, it is not favored by quite as many birds as black oil sunflower. However, birds with larger bills, such as cardinals and jays, happily eat it. Striped sunflower is used in many birdseed mixes.

How to offer: It is best offered in hanging tubular feeders, hopper feeders, and tray feeders that are mounted above the ground.

Birds attracted: Appeals to the same birds as black oil sunflower seed — chickadees, titmice, nuthatches, goldfinches, House Finches, cardinals, grosbeaks, and jays.

Striped sunflower seed

HULLED SUNFLOWER SEED

This is sunflower seeds without the hulls. It comes as either complete hulled seeds, often called "sunflower hearts," or broken up into very small pieces, often called "sunflower chips." It may come from either black oil or striped sunflower. One of the big advan-

Hulled sunflower seed

tages of using hulled sunflower is that there are no messy shells to clean up under the feeder. Therefore, it is very useful for feeding on patios, on decks, in gardens, or in any other areas where you do not want sunflower hulls to accumulate. Hulled sunflower, since it lacks the protection of the hull, is more apt to mold if it gets wet. Check feeders regularly and keep them filled with fresh dry seed. If you live in a very wet climate, you may want to feed sunflower with the shell on.

Hulled sunflower is used by more species of birds than any other seed, because the shells are already removed and there is less work and energy spent to open the shells. Goldfinches love it. This seed will also attract some birds that do not usually eat sunflower, or find it hard to crack the shells, such as Carolina Wrens, mockingbirds, bluebirds, and Pine Warblers.

How to offer: This is best offered in a large-hole tubular feeder. It can also be offered in hopper feeders. People often put an umbrella-like baffle over tube feeders to help keep the seed dry.

Birds attracted: This appeals to a greater variety of birds than sunflower with the hulls on, because birds that normally could not crack open the shell can eat it. These include mockingbirds, wrens, and woodpeckers, along with chickadees, titmice, nuthatches, goldfinches, House Finches, cardinals, grosbeaks, sparrows, and jays.

THISTLE (NYJER®) SEED

Thistle is a very tiny black seed. It does not come from our wildflower called thistle but is imported from Africa, Asia, and India. Its scientific name is *Guizotia abyssinica* and its agricultural name is niger seed. In part to help people distinguish it from the wildflower, thistle seed

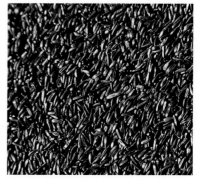

Thistle (Nyjer) seed

is now being called Nyjer seed. The name Nyjer is trademarked by the Wild Bird Feeding Institute (comprised of companies in the bird-feeding industry), which encourages its use. This seed is sterilized by heat treatment when it is imported to North America so that any weed seeds that may have gotten incorporated with it will not germinate under the feeder. Nyjer should be kept dry, as it may mold in wet conditions. Birds may not eat Nyjer if it is not fresh, so you may want to buy it in smaller quantities, in amounts your birds will consume quickly.

Sometimes this seed is mixed with finely chopped sunflower chips and other small seeds such as canary seed and millet in a "finch mix," which is more economical than straight Nyjer.

How to offer: Since thistle/Nyjer is so tiny, it must be offered in special tube feeders that have small seed portals so that it does not all spill out (see page 31). It can also be offered in feeders with very fine wire mesh, or sometimes "thistle socks" — little bags of porous cloth out of which birds can peck the seeds.

Birds attracted: This is one of the top favorites of goldfinches and other members of the finch family, such as House Finches, Purple Finches, Lesser

---

STORING AND POURING SEED

Seed should be stored in a dry, cool place in containers with tight-fitting lids. Seed stored under optimum conditions can last 8–12 months or longer. Improperly stored seed can become moldy, or grain moths can occur. Large metal trash cans and other containers work well for seed storage. If seed is stored outdoors, make sure container lids are firmly secured to prevent raccoons and squirrels from getting in.

Many people use commercially available seed scoops to scoop the seed out of large bags. We have found that plastic juice pitchers minus the lids work well. Commercially made seed pitchers are also available.

Goldfinches, Lawrence's Finches, Pine Siskins, and redpolls. Even chickadees and sometimes other species will eat this seed. A big advantage of this seed is that squirrels usually do not eat it, and some of the less favorite feeder birds, such as grackles, cannot eat the seed through the tiny holes of the feeders.

MILLET

Millet is a small round seed about the size of the head of a pin. There are several different types. White proso millet is light-colored and the most popular with birds. Red and golden millet are colored as named, not quite as favored by birds, and less available in stores.

Millet

Millet is most often sold as part of a seed mix, often as a major component. In some stores it is possible to buy straight millet.

How to offer: Seed mixes containing millet can be placed in a variety of feeders, such as hanging tubular feeders, hopper feeders, and tray feeders hung or placed on the ground. Straight millet is best offered in hopper or platform feeders.

Birds attracted: Millet is especially liked by ground-feeding species such as doves, sparrows and juncos, bobwhites, and quails. Cardinals and buntings also like millet. In some regions, Indigo and Painted Buntings can be attracted to feeders filled with just white proso millet.

SAFFLOWER SEED

Safflower is a white oval seed that is about half the size of a black oil sunflower seed. It has a rich oil content and is continuing to gain in popularity. One of the biggest advantages of safflower is that it is usually not eaten by squirrels or grackles — species which people often try to discourage from feeders.

Safflower seed may get a mixed reception from regular feeder birds; some seem to accept it immediately, others take a while to warm up to it, and some will not eat it. If it is mixed with other seeds, birds may more readily accept it. Many "cardinal mixes" contain safflower and sunflower seed.

How to offer: It is best offered in hanging tube feeders, hopper feeders, and tray feeders.

Birds attracted: Safflower appeals to many of the same birds as black oil sunflower seed. These include chickadees, titmice, nuthatches, goldfinches, House Finches, grosbeaks, and jays. Cardinals are particularly fond of this seed.

Safflower seed

CRACKED CORN

Most corn offered as birdseed comes as cracked corn — dried corn kernels that have been cracked into smaller pieces. Cracked corn is sometimes available by itself but is more usually found in seed mixes. It is less expensive than seeds like sunflower, safflower,

Cracked corn

and thistle/Nyjer. Since it is cracked, it is more susceptible to mold if it gets wet, so keep feeders clean and dry, and remove any moldy seed. If using it in tray feeders, be sure they have screen bottoms so the water will drain and the seed will dry.

How to offer: Cracked corn is best offered in seed mixes in tubes, hopper feeders, or tray feeders. If using it alone, offer it in tray feeders placed on the ground.

Birds attracted: A wide variety of birds that like to feed on the ground come to cracked corn. These include pheasants, quails, doves, sparrows, towhees, blackbirds, grackles, and jays.

MILO

Milo, also called sorghum, is a small, round, red seed that is twice the size of a millet seed and is often fed to livestock and poultry. High in carbohydrates, this inexpensive seed is one of the main components of cheaper birdseed mixes. Milo is lower on the list of seed prefer-

Milo

ences for most birds, especially species that feed above the ground, such as chickadees; however, milo is accepted by ground-feeding species like doves, sparrows, quails, and towhees. In general, when mixes with a high percentage of milo are offered in tube feeders, birds will toss the milo out onto the ground as they look for seeds they like better, such as sunflower. The ground-feeding birds then often eat the milo and other seed that has been scattered out of the feeders.

According to older studies of birds, milo was thought to be undesirable to most birds. But recent studies of birds' seed preferences have shown that a number of birds — especially western species like Steller's Jays, California Towhees, Gambel's Quails, and White-crowned Sparrows — readily eat milo. Some people think that, over time, birds adapt to eat what is offered to them and that more species of birds may be learning to accept milo.

How to offer: Milo in most cases is used as an ingredient in less expensive birdseed mixes, which can be offered in tube, hopper, or tray feeders.

Birds attracted: Mostly appeals to species that will feed on the ground, such as doves, jays, sparrows, grackles, and quails. Seems to be more accepted by western bird species.

BIRDSEED MIXES

There are numerous kinds of birdseed mixes now available, including mixes designed to selectively attract certain species.

The main ingredients in birdseed mixes are sunflower, millet, peanut pieces, safflower, cracked corn, and milo. The most expensive of these are peanuts, sunflower, and safflower. Millet is of medium expense, and corn and milo are the cheapest ingredients. The cost of the seed mix depends on the proportions of seeds used.

Since sunflower is the most desired seed, and one of the most expensive, quality seed mixes that contain more sunflower attract a lot of birds but are also more expensive. Mixes with high proportions of milo, corn, and millet are cheaper and in general will attract fewer varieties of birds. There are some

High-quality mixed seed

exceptions, such as the fact that many western bird species tend to readily accept milo. We have visited western states such as Arizona where people feed birds straight milo and get many species at their feeders.

Inexpensive mixed seed

Finch mix

the sunflower, tossing the millet, milo, and corn to the ground, where the ground-feeding species will get it.

Ground-feeding species, such as Mourning Doves, sparrows, juncos, towhees, and quails, readily eat less expensive seeds like cracked corn, milo, and millet and thus will be attracted to the less expensive seed, which is best offered nearer ground level.

How to offer: Higher-quality, more expensive mixes that contain more sunflower should be offered in tube, hopper, or platform feeders mounted above the ground. Cheaper, lower-quality mixes are best offered in tray feeders near or on the ground.

Birds attracted: Chickadees, nuthatches, finches, cardinals, grosbeaks, and titmice generally feed above the ground and prefer sunflower seed and, therefore, will come to the more expensive mixes that contain a higher percentage of sunflower seed. These birds often pick through seed mixes and eat

SUET

Suet is a top favorite of woodpeckers, as well as chickadees, nuthatches, and many other birds, and should be part of a good feeding station setup. It is a type of hard white fat that comes from near the kidneys of cows. Birds love the pure fat of suet, since it gives them lots of calories ounce for ounce to fuel their high metabolisms. Suet comes raw or rendered (cooked and cooled).

You can buy raw suet from supermarkets, although it is not always available. People offer raw suet in mesh onion bags, or pound it into holes that have been drilled into logs or wood. One word of caution: do not use raw suet in hot weather, for it can turn rancid and may also easily melt.

Some people render their own suet, a smelly process, by cutting it into chunks, slowly melting it, then cooling it. Often people add other ingredients to their homemade suet, such as peanut butter or chopped nuts, mixed birdseed, raisins, and other fruit. Or sometimes people make their own homemade bird "pudding" by using lard or vegetable shortening instead of suet, and

A suet cake

mixing in ingredients like cornmeal, peanut butter, birdseed, chopped fruit and nuts, and so forth.

Convenient commercial suet cakes of many sizes and flavors are now readily available at stores selling bird-feeding supplies. Their big advantage is that they have already been rendered (i.e., cooked and cooled with impurities strained out), usually twice. They are less likely to melt or go rancid than raw suet. Keep them in the refrigerator for easy removal from their packaging.

Commercial cakes appeal to a wide variety of avian palates and come in many delicious flavors, such as peanut, berry, orange, apple, pecan, or mixed seed, and some even have calcium or dried insect parts added. Birds such as wrens, bluebirds, and warblers, which may not come to birdseed, are often lured to commercial suet cakes.

How to offer: Suet cakes are offered in wire mesh holders. Some hopper-type bird feeders come equipped with wire suet holders on their sides. Keep suet out of the reach of squirrels by hanging it on poles that have squirrel baffles. Some suet holders come surrounded by a larger cage that will keep out starlings, grackles, and large birds but allow chickadees and other small birds to enter through the holes in the cage. There is a "starling-resistant" suet holder that has a wooden roof, so that the only way to reach the suet is by clinging or hovering underneath. The theory is that birds like woodpeckers and chickadees can accomplish this but large birds cannot. This often works, but we have heard of some clever grackles and Western Scrub-Jays that have learned to flutter up and grab the suet.

In hot weather keep suet cakes in the shade to prevent melting. For extremely hot weather, there is a type of suet "dough" cake formulated for summer feeding. It has less fat, and flour or meal has been added to raise its melting point.

Birds attracted: A favorite of all the woodpeckers, such as Downy, Hairy, Red-bellied, and even Pileated Woodpeckers, as well as chickadees, titmice, nuthatches, starlings, and grackles. Unusual feeder birds like Pine Warblers, Carolina Wrens, Brown Creepers, and bluebirds may also visit suet.

SUGAR WATER

Sugar water is offered to birds because it mimics the composition of nectar in flowers, which many birds naturally drink. Hummingbirds and orioles make a habit of it, but up to fifty other species have also been recorded at sugar water feeders. You can easily make your own sugar water solution. Use white table sugar — *not* brown sugar, artificial sweetener, or honey — and mix four parts water to one part sugar. Place in a pan and boil 1–2 minutes. Cool and then place in a suitable feeder. Store the unused portion in the refrigerator.

Sugar solution is very susceptible to molding in warm weather, and this mold can be bad for the birds. In warm weather (temperatures over 60 degrees) be sure to change the solution every

2–3 days to keep it fresh and free of mold.

How to offer: Sugar water solution should be placed in a special hummingbird or oriole feeder. For more on these feeders, see page 42.

Birds attracted: Hummingbirds, orioles, finches, woodpeckers, jays, chickadees, titmice, tanagers, wrens, mockingbirds, warblers, and many others.

PEANUTS, PEANUT BUTTER, AND OTHER NUTS

Peanuts are becoming increasingly popular as a feeder food. They are relished by many birds because they are a high-protein, oil-rich food. Peanuts are often used in birdseed mixes, usually broken in half or into pieces. Peanut hearts are the small center of the peanut and do not have as desirable a taste to

Shelled peanuts

birds as the rest of the peanut, so they are not as popular in bird feeding.

Peanuts may also be offered by themselves, generally whole and out of their shells. Less frequently, people offer them in their shells, but only very adept birds, like jays and titmice, can get them out of the shell. Do not buy cocktail peanuts from the supermarket; they are expensive and have a high salt content. Most commonly people buy shelled peanuts in bulk from stores that sell bird-feeding supplies.

In hot humid weather peanuts can be subject to mold. So in these conditions, check frequently to make sure they are fresh and only put out what the birds will eat quickly. Needless to say, squirrels are very fond of peanuts, so place peanut feeders out of the reach of squirrels.

Birds also relish peanut butter. Most people offer it in homemade recipes for "bird puddings," combining it with birdseed, cornmeal, and other ingredients and then stuffing it into pine cones or logs with holes drilled in them.

Other nuts tend to be expensive items for bird feeding. Nevertheless, an increasing array of tree nuts such as pecans are being used as additions to the better birdseed mixes and used in suet cake recipes. These can help attract a variety of birds such as Carolina Wrens, flickers, and Red-bellied Woodpeckers.

How to offer whole shelled peanuts: Put the whole shelled peanuts in special feeders that are basically cylinders of 1/4-inch wire mesh, available in bird stores. These ingenious feeders prevent large birds from carrying the peanuts away whole and allow the smaller birds like wrens and chickadees to peck bite-sized pieces out of the wire cage.

Birds attracted: Woodpeckers, flickers, chickadees, wrens, titmice, nuthatches, jays.

A number of bird species like fruit, and it is fun to experiment with different types of fruit to see who will come. Fruit is generally used for warm-weather feeding. Keep it fresh and discard any that has become moldy.

Oranges, apples, and grape jelly for birds

Orange halves will attract orioles, Red-bellied Woodpeckers, tanagers, and others. Put them on platforms or attach to fruit holders (see page 41).

Grape jelly is attractive to orioles and catbirds. Offer it in a little dish on a platform.

Raisins will be eaten by robins, mockingbirds, bluebirds, jays, woodpeckers, and others. Some people soften the raisins in warm water first and then sprinkle them on a tray feeder, picnic table, or window ledge.

People also feed a variety of other fruits, such as blueberries, cut-up apples, and grapes, which are eaten by orioles, mockingbirds, robins, and more.

MEALWORMS

Mealworms are smooth brown ¾-inch-long larvae from a type of grain beetle called *Tenebrio molitor*. Mealworms have a big potential and are gaining in popularity as a bird food. They are available from pet stores, wild bird stores, and by mail order (see Resources).

Male Eastern Bluebird with mealworms from a feeder

They are sold in plastic containers and can be stored for 3–12 months in the refrigerator, where they will remain dormant. People usually buy them in quantities of up to 500, or even more if they have lots of birds that love them. One of the advantages of mealworms is that they are a "live" food, and many birds that never come to seeds will love them. They are a favorite of bluebirds, and many bluebird enthusiasts now offer them during the bluebird nesting season. A large variety of birds may come to them, like thrushes, mocking-birds, wrens, and warblers, as well as feeder regulars.

How to offer: Feed when the weather is warm, not freezing. It is best to put them in a small to medium-sized dish with steeply sloping sides; otherwise they can crawl out of the dish. Since birds eagerly gobble up mealworms,

and since it is impractical to supply an endless amount all day, it may make sense to offer a limited amount at the same time each day. Birds will then come to expect them at that time.

Birds attracted: Bluebirds, mocking-birds, thrashers, wrens, cardinals, jays, titmice, warblers, thrushes, and potentially virtually any bird that eats insects.

A WORD ABOUT BAKED GOODS

Stale bread and other baked goods should not be the main fare offered at most feeder stations, for they do not have the nutritional value of most birdseed. Nevertheless, people do offer crumbled baked goods and table scraps to birds. Crows are especially fond of these items. If you do put out such foods, make sure none of it is moldy or spoiled.

TUBE FEEDERS

One of the most basic types of bird feeder consists of a long cylindrical tube with holes, or portals, in it where the birds can get to the seed. Most of these feeders have tubes of clear plastic or tough polyvinyl, but a few are made of metal or ceramics. There are also wood feeders based on this same principle. They are usually square towers with two wood sides and two clear plastic sides.

There are two basic types of tube feeders: those with tiny feeding holes, for small seeds, and those with large holes, for larger seeds. Be sure to pick the one for the seed that you are going to offer.

SMALL-HOLE, OR "FINCH," TUBULAR FEEDERS

These feeders are designed to hold small seeds, such as thistle/Nyjer or finch mixes. The portals, or openings into the tube, are small and oblong in these feeders. If they were larger, the seed would fall right out. These feeders

Finch feeder, showing the small holes for the small seeds

Small-hole (or "finch") tubular feeder

can be used by small birds; larger birds, such as cardinals and jays, may have trouble getting any seed out of them. They are often called finch feeders, since finches especially like these types of seeds, but chickadees and titmice will also visit these feeders.

Large-hole tubular feeder, with large seed portals

LARGE-HOLE TUBULAR FEEDERS

These feeders are designed to hold larger seeds, such as sunflower and mixed seeds. The large seed portals are about ½ inch or more in diameter and usually have a baffle inside the feeder to allow an even flow of seed to the portal. They are attractive to most species of feeder birds, large or small.

KEY FEATURES TO LOOK FOR

When buying a tube feeder, key features to consider are the amount of seed the feeder holds, the number and type of portals it has, the ease of filling, and ease of cleaning.

Size — Smaller tube feeders hold less seed. They can be a good start for someone new to the hobby, but once they begin to attract birds, the feeder will be emptied frequently. When this happens, you may want to consider getting a tube that will hold enough seed to last for several days. This can be one that is either taller or with a larger diameter.

Large-capacity tube feeder

If there are times when you are unable to tend your feeders for a day or two because of travel or business, try to get a really large feeder so that there will be seed in it for several days. Of course, another solution is to get many tubular feeders and fill them all or to have a friend fill your feeders while you are away.

Some feeders combine several tubes into one feeder. This may allow you to use different types of seed in each tube to see which the birds prefer. It also, obviously, holds more seed.

Number of Portals — The portals are the holes in the feeder tube where the birds come to get the seeds. The number of portals determines the number of birds you can accommodate at one time. Many small birds, like chickadees and titmice, come to the feeders only briefly, just to get a seed and then leave. These

Tube feeder with four portals

birds do not tie up the feeders with long visits. On the other hand, goldfinches and other finches tend to come to a feeder and stay there as they feed, sometimes for minutes at a time. Because of this, if you have a feeder with just two or four portals, you can only attract that many goldfinches at a time. To attract more goldfinches, choose feeders with more portals or put up several tube feeders. You can also use tubes made of wire mesh; since smaller birds can cling to the wire mesh, this feeder can accommodate many birds at once.

Ease of Filling — One thing you will be doing a lot is filling feeders. Be sure that the tubular feeder you get is easy to fill. When you are looking to buy one, open the top and imagine yourself trying to fill it. It should be easy to pour seed into, and the top should fit down snugly after filling.

Ease of Cleaning — To clean tube feeders, use a long bottle brush. The bottoms of some tube feeders can be removed by undoing a few screws; this can help you clean the lower portion of the tube.

ACCESSORIES

You can often buy trays that will attach to the bottom of tubular feeders and catch most seeds or shells that the birds drop out of the feeder. Trays can be helpful in limiting hulls under a feeder where you have plantings or in an apartment situation where you do not want any shells to fall on other peoples' balconies.

When feeding hulled sunflower, the tray has the advantage of collecting bits of good sunflower seed that the birds may discard at first but then eat from the tray. Trays are also good when you

Tray attachment to a tubular feeder

do not want to attract mammals such as raccoons to your feeder area.

The other advantage of a tray beneath a tube feeder is that it provides a larger perching area. Larger birds, such as cardinals and grosbeaks, that may have difficulty clinging to small perches will more comfortably feed from the tray.

The basic design of a hopper, or ranch, feeder is to have a seed compartment that regulates the flow of seed onto a feeding platform. These feeders are most often in the style of a wooden ranch, a little house, or gazebo with glass or plastic on the sides. You usually

Hopper, or ranch, feeder

fill a hopper feeder from the top, either by lifting up the whole roof or by lifting up one side of a hinged roof.

The advantage of hopper feeders is that they present the seed on a platform that provides a larger and wider perching area than just straight perches. Many species of birds that prefer to feed on the ground will also come to hopper feeders. These include cardinals, grosbeaks, sparrows, juncos, doves, and others.

KEY FEATURES TO LOOK FOR

The main things to look for in a good ranch, or hopper, feeder are seed capacity, area of the tray for feeding, and ease of filling.

Seed Capacity — Look closely at how much seed you can put into any hopper feeder you buy. Since many birds can feed at once at these feeders, the seed may go down quickly, so you may want to get one with a large capacity.

Tray Area — The size of the platform attached to a hopper feeder is critical in determining which birds can use it. The tray must be large enough to fit medium-sized birds such as cardinals, grosbeaks, jays, and doves comfortably. This will maximize your chances of getting as many species as possible. There should also be drainage holes in the platform so the seed stays dry.

Ease of Filling — Check the hopper feeders you are looking at to see how easy they are to fill. The best kind have a hinged roof that folds back. Be sure this is well made and will hold up to frequent use.

Hopper feeder with suet holders

ACCESSORIES

Some hopper feeders have suet baskets attached to one or both ends. This can be a nice addition, for it attracts more species to the feeder and offers many different foods at the same spot.

TRAYS AND GROUND FEEDERS

Many species of birds prefer to feed on or near the ground, for this is the way they find the majority of their food in the wild. This includes all of the doves and sparrows, as well as cardinals, towhees, blackbirds, jays, pheasants, and

Tray feeder with mixed seed on the ground

many others. Some of these species, such as cardinals and blackbirds, are adaptable enough that they may accept coming to hopper or tube feeders, but other species, such as sparrows, usually stay on the ground.

Some people just sprinkle seed on the ground in an open area that is

cleared of vegetation. However, seed sprinkled directly on the ground is susceptible to moisture and molding. A better approach is to place the seed in a tray. Trays usually have four wooden sides with a screen or mesh

Tray feeder with mixed seed hung from a pole

Blue Jays are one species that often feeds on the ground

bottom to let rain drain through and keep the seed dry. Trays can be placed just off the ground (they should be on legs or another support to keep them a few inches off the ground), mounted on a pole, or hung from your feeder poles or a tree.

Trays are very versatile feeders, and most seed mixes and large seeds can be placed in them. You can also use them to offer many specialty items, such as fruits, jelly, and mealworms. Just about any bird can come to a tray feeder.

SUET FEEDERS

There are a variety of suet feeders available, depending on the form of suet you are using. If using raw suet from the meat market, which is often still available if you ask at the meat counter, it can be hung in a string or plastic mesh bag. It can also be cut into chunks and pressed or hammered into holes drilled into a log. Then the log can be hung off a feeder pole or branch.

If you are using suet cakes, they can be placed in small wire baskets, which are then hung off a feeder pole or branch. Some baskets are attached to additional pieces of wood that may extend down below the suet cage; the wood provides a support for woodpeckers to brace their tails against as they hold on to the wire mesh. Sometimes, two suet cages are attached to one board, and this allows you to put

Suet in a wire holder

Downy Woodpecker at a suet holder nailed to a tree

Upside-down suet feeder

out blocks of different flavors to offer variety to the birds.

You can hang these suet cages off an existing pole setup with other feeders, or hang them off a branch or house eaves. Some people even just attach them to a tree. To prevent squirrels and raccoons from reaching them, hang them off poles that have baffles.

Suet cages are often attached to other feeders, especially at the ends of ranch feeders. This offers "one-stop shopping" for visiting birds.

Suet in a protective cage

Several suet feeder types try to limit access to the suet. There is an upside-down suet feeder that consists of a little roof with a suet cage underneath it. Certain less desirable birds, such as starlings, have trouble hanging on upside down and so may be discouraged from feeding on the suet. Smaller birds and woodpeckers have no problem with this, although they may take a little time to discover the suet under the roof.

Another type consists of a suet cage placed inside a larger cage. This is supposed to prevent access by large birds such as crows and grackles and also by squirrels. These visitors cannot reach through the larger cage to get at the suet, but all of the regular feeder visitors that are smaller can get right through.

OTHER FEEDER DESIGNS

DISH FEEDERS

Some types of feeders are just a simple dish that can be hung or mounted. Sometimes these have a cover over the dish, like a small dome. This dome is sometimes designed to keep the seed dry, and in other examples it can serve as a squirrel baffle as well. Dish feeders are much like tray feeders, although they are usually smaller and may not hold as much seed. A few models enable you to adjust the height of the dome over the dish. This limits the size of birds that can use the feeder; if the cover is low, only smaller birds can get in.

ORNAMENTAL AND DECORATIVE FEEDERS

There are many other styles of feeders that are variations on the themes of tube and hopper feeders. When purchasing these feeders, just be sure that they accomplish what you want with regard to feeding the birds. They should hold seed well, dispense it in a way that the birds can easily feed, be easy to fill, and be made to last.

Dome and dish feeder

A decorative sunflower seed feeder

WINDOW FEEDERS

There are two basic types of window feeders: those that you place on the window glass and those that are actually placed in the window opening. Feeders placed on windows are almost always attached by means of suction cups and are made of clear materials or have a clear back so that you can see the birds come to feed. You can buy hummingbird feeders, little tray feeders, tube feeders, and even hopper feeders that attach to your window.

Some larger feeders are more like a box that is placed across the sill of the open window, and then the window is pulled down to fit snugly on top of it. A clear back allows you to see the birds that come to feed on the large tray area that is open to the outdoors. In some models, the back is made of a one-way see-through material, so you can see the birds but they cannot see you and possibly be scared away.

Window feeders are perfect for seeing birds up close. In our experience, they do not increase window hits by the birds (see page 61). If you are just starting to feed birds, begin by using other types of feeders and place them near trees or shrubs birds frequent. Once birds are comfortable coming to these feeders, you will have a better chance of their discovering any window feeders you may put up.

A window tray feeder

FEEDERS FOR SPECIALIZED FOODS

There are many different kinds of foods that you can offer birds. A few of them require specialized feeders. These include nuts, fruit, sugar water, thistle, mealworms, and jelly.

NUT FEEDERS

A variety of nuts (peanuts, pecans, and so forth), either whole or in pieces, can be offered to birds. Nuts in pieces can be offered in large-seed tubular feeders and they will flow easily to the portals. Nuts that are whole or in large pieces will not work as well in these feeders and are best placed in a coarse wire mesh feeder that contains the nuts but lets the birds peck at the nuts through the mesh. These feeders are often a cylinder of wire mesh, with or without

A wire mesh peanut feeder

perches. Or they can be partially wooden feeders with wire mesh in the sides.

FRUIT FEEDERS

Fruits that can be fed to birds include large fruits such as apples and oranges, which can be eaten by orioles, catbirds, woodpeckers, and tanagers. The fruits

Baltimore Oriole at a fruit feeder

are generally cut into halves, which are then pushed onto pegs or spikes of some kind. The "feeder" can be as simple as a nail in a tree or a vertical piece of wood with a wooden peg coming out both sides. Large fruits can also be placed on tray feeders.

Smaller fruits like berries and raisins may be offered on a tray feeder or in a small dish.

SUGAR WATER FEEDERS

Sugar water attracts a wide variety of birds but is usually set out to attract orioles and hummingbirds. It should be placed in a sugar water feeder, of which there are two types. One type is a simple dish with a cover and holes in the cover where birds can get at the nectar. The cover lifts off for easy filling and cleaning. There are also perches around the outside.

Dish-type hummingbird feeder

The other type is basically a bottle turned upside-down into a dish. These can hold more liquid than the dish type and are particularly helpful in areas that get lots of hummingbirds. Oriole feeders are usually orange and hum-mingbird feeders are usually red. Keep all sugar water feeders very clean by scrubbing them with hot water and, if needed, a little vinegar. Rinse well. Specialized hummingbird feeder brushes make cleaning these feeders easier.

A bottle-type hummingbird feeder

For information on sugar water solutions, see page 27.

Note that when you offer sweet foods such as sugar water solutions, fruit, or jelly, you may potentially attract ants. The easiest way to protect your feeders from ants is to use an ant guard. This is a small plastic cup with a hook in the center and another hook hanging underneath. Fill the cup with water, then hang the ant guard from the feeder pole and the feeder from the bottom of the guard. As ants crawl up the pole and down toward the feeder they encounter the little moat of water and are stopped. Some sugar water feeders have a built-in ant guard at their top.

THISTLE SOCKS

We have talked about tube feeders that hold thistle/Nyjer, but you can also buy fine mesh bags, or socks, for this purpose. You simply pour the seed into the bag and hang the bag from your feeder pole. The seeds just barely poke through the mesh, and the birds will land on the bag and eat the seed.

A thistle sock with thistle in it

MEALWORMS

Many species of birds love to eat mealworms, and there are a variety of ways to offer them. The mealworms usually need to be placed in some contained

A male Eastern Bluebird visits a dome feeder offering mealworms

area so that they do not crawl out. You can use a small straight-sided dish that is placed on a tray feeder, or you can use a small tray feeder with a dome above it, which will keep them both dry and contained.

For more information on mealworms, see page 30.

JELLY

Many birds like to eat jelly, especially grape jelly. These include catbirds, orioles, and tanagers. Offer grape jelly in a small dish that is placed in a tray feeder. You may need an ant guard to keep ants off the feeder. See sugar water feeders, page 42.

SETTING UP FEEDERS

SETTING UP FEEDERS

Every feeder has to be placed somewhere. In this section we tell you when, how, and where to set up feeders in your yard. For related issues about the safety of birds near feeders, see Solving Feeder Problems, p. 58.

WHEN

The best time to put up your bird feeders is now! Do not wait. Any seed feeder can be put up at any time of year for the birds. There is a common misconception that you should start feeding birds in fall and stop in spring. Fall is actually when there is the most food available for birds in the wild. All the seeds and fruits have matured and insects are abundant as well. Spring, on the other hand, is when there is the least food available to the birds. Seeds

and fruits have been eaten, new ones have not yet been produced, and insects have yet to come out in full force.

The best course is to feed the birds all year round. They will benefit from it, and you will enjoy seeing them in every month. The only exception to this is offering sugar water solutions. If the hummingbirds leave your area for the winter, then take down your sugar water feeders when the last one has gone.

HOW

Except for a few tray feeders, most bird feeders need to be placed well above the ground. This involves either mounting from beneath or hanging from above.

One of the best ways to put up feeders is to use a metal pole that has one or more hooks off the top. These poles are available at bird-feeding stores or at

Goldfinches on a tube feeder with hulled sunflower

You can mount many feeders off the same pole

garden centers. The pole should sink securely in the ground to be sure that it is sturdy. Many pole systems have a separate bottom sleeve section with an auger at the tip that literally screws into the ground. The above-ground pole then slips into this. Other poles may have several points that all sink into the ground for rigidity; generally all you need to do is press these extensions into the ground with your foot.

Some poles have one hook at the top from which you can hang a feeder. Other systems have ways to attach several hooks to the top of the pole. This is very advantageous, because it enables you to hang a variety of feeders at the same place. A single pole with many hooks also enables you to protect all the feeders from squirrels with a single baffle around the pole. (See Squirrel-Proofing, page 49.)

This branch hook can go over a branch or be used as an extender on a pole

Some poles have a mounting flange at the top which you can attach to the bottom of a feeder with screws. This is an excellent way to mount a single large ranch feeder.

You can also hang feeders from tree branches or eaves of houses. A branch hook makes it easy to hang a feeder from a tree. A large hook at one end goes over the branch, and a smaller hook at the other end holds the feeder. Extension hooks of various lengths allow you to hang the feeder at any height you choose; they are like long S-hooks. These same extension hooks can be used along with an eye-hook underneath the eaves of a house to hang the feeder in front of a window where you can see the birds.

If you have a deck, you can mount feeders off the railing, although if you have squirrels you need to take certain steps (see Squirrel-Proofing, page 49). There are clamp hooks that will attach to the railing and that have an arm with a hook at the end from which you can hang a feeder. Birdbaths can be attached in the same way.

You can also attach a feeder to a bracket mounted on the side of a building.

WHERE

In most cases, you will eventually want to place your feeders so that you can easily watch the birds. This may be near a porch or patio or outside a window of your house from which you often look out, such as over a kitchen sink or in an office or family room.

But if you are just starting out feeding birds, you need to get the birds to find the feeders. The best way to do this is to first put the feeders near an area of your property where you often see birds. If there are some trees or shrubby locations where you have seen birds, start by placing feeders near these areas. This will maximize the chances that the birds will find your feeders

Feeders placed near protective cover for the birds

quickly. Once birds have found your feeders, you can gradually move the feeders, 20–30 feet at a time, nearer to the house so that you can better see the birds. When you have been feeding birds for a while, you can usually put feeders just about anywhere and the birds will find them.

It is good to have some places for birds to perch, such as trees, within 50 feet of the feeders. This allows them to come and go from the feeder to the perches as needed and to wait safely until the feeder is free. An open space of at least 20 feet in diameter around the base of the feeder is preferable, for it allows birds to feed on the fallen seed and to see any predators, such as cats, that might be nearby (for more on dealing with cats see page 65). Some shrubbery near the feeder is also good as protective cover that birds can dive into, in case they see a hawk.

MAINTAINING FEEDERS

Be sure to keep feeders of all kinds clean and free from mold and insects. Cleaning up your feeders will make them safer for the birds and can really improve the overall appearance of your feeding station.

Regularly inspect your feeders to see that seed hulls are removed and that no mold is growing on old uneaten seed. Take feeders apart, clean out old seed, and scrub the feeder with hot soapy water. Rinse thoroughly. Some feeders come apart for easy cleaning, others may need a screwdriver or other tools to open up.

There are many good brushes on the market for cleaning feeders. Use the long bottle brushes to help clean the inside of tubular feeders; tiny brushes are available for cleaning out the portals of sugar water feeders. Be sure seed feeders are completely dry before adding fresh food.

It is also a good idea to frequently clean up the area under the feeders by raking up old seeds and debris. Occasionally move feeders to new locations to reduce the buildup of debris in any one area.

Squirrel-Proofing

For almost anybody who feeds birds, one of the top questions on their mind is "How do I keep squirrels off my feeder?" Some people actually think that it is impossible, but this is far from the truth. There are many things you can do to reduce squirrels at your feeders and, in most cases, keep them off altogether. If you like squirrels and like birds, there are ways to offer squirrels food with separate feeders so they do not disturb the birds.

The source of the problem is that squirrels eat seeds in the wild. When you offer seeds to birds, squirrels are attracted. If they get on your feeders, they eat a lot of seed and can keep the birds away simply by monopolizing the feeders.

The abilities of squirrels are tremendous. Below is a list of the key abilities you have to keep in mind when squirrel-proofing your feeders. Also remember, they have 24 hours a day to think about how to get to your

Squirrels — you can protect your feeders from them

IMPORTANT SQUIRREL ABILITIES TO KEEP IN MIND

♦ They can jump straight up 4–5 feet.
♦ They can jump straight out or out and down 12 feet, sometimes more.
♦ They can climb up any pole and down or along any wire.

---

feeders, while you may have only an hour or two a week to figure out how to keep them off!

There are three main ways to approach keeping squirrels off your feeders. One is to place some barrier, or baffle, they cannot cross between them and the feeder. Another is to use feeder designs that make it impossible for the squirrels to get to the seed even if they reach the feeder. Finally, you can change the foods you offer to those that squirrels do not favor.

BAFFLING THE SQUIRRELS

IMPORTANT NOTE — Baffles are only effective in situations where you can place the feeder 5 feet off the ground and 12 feet or more from anyplace from which the squirrel can jump, such as a tree or shrub, roof, or deck. This usually means out in a very open area of lawn. If you do not have this situation, then baffles are not likely to solve your problem and you need to try the other two options.

If you do have an open area of sufficient size, the best approach is to place your feeders 5½ feet or more high on a metal pole and then put a baffle on the pole. There are basically two types of pole baffles: stovepipes and cones or domes.

A stovepipe baffle

STOVEPIPE BAFFLES

These long, cylindrical baffles are very effective. The best are 12–24 inches long, about 6 inches in diameter, and covered at the top. They need to be placed on the pole so that the top of the baffle is at least 5 feet above the ground; this way a squirrel cannot just jump to the top of the baffle from the ground. The squirrel will climb up the pole and usually end up inside the pipe, not be able to get through, and then back down. The baffle is too large in diameter and too slippery for the squirrel to hold on to. What generally happens is that the squirrels try for a while and then just give up. They may feed on seed that drops below the feeders, but this does not disturb the birds very much. Longer stovepipe baffles keep raccoons off feeders as well.

It is also important to keep your feeders well above the bottom edge of the baffle, for you do not want the squirrels to climb the pole to the bottom edge of the baffle and then try to jump up to the feeders.

CONE OR DOME BAFFLES

Cone baffles achieve the same result as stovepipe baffles and are also placed on

poles 4–5 feet above the ground. They work slightly differently. In this case the squirrels cannot reach around the baffle to get above it. The baffle should be at least 14–16 inches in diameter in order to keep the squirrels from getting around it. Some baffles are metal and others are clear plastic; both work well.

A metal cone baffle that wraps around the pole

A tubular feeder placed high into a dome

Some metal baffles can actually be snapped around the pole. This is especially useful if the pole is a shepherd's crook, where the curve at the top of the pole makes it impossible to slide a baffle over. It is also helpful because you don't have to take down your feeders in order to put the baffle around the pole.

Dome baffles can be mounted above or below the feeder. Some people try to hang feeders from tree branches or from a wire strung between two trees and then put a dome baffle just above the feeder. In this case, the squirrels may try to climb down the wire and then slowly slide over the edge of the baffle and catch the feeder beneath on their way down. One way to prevent this is to get a larger dome and place the feeder high up into the dome. Make sure the feeder is 12 feet from any tree trunk from which a squirrel could jump.

If you do not have a large open space in which to place a pole with a stovepipe baffle, you can control squirrels through the feeders you use and through the foods that you offer. Some feeders are designed to prevent squirrels from getting to the food, even if they get on the feeder. These can be used in situations where it is impossible to baffle the squirrels. There are three designs: feeders within cages, feeders with spring-loaded openings, and mechanical devices.

CAGES

Tubular feeders can be placed within a larger cylinder of wire mesh that is about 1–1½ inches square. This enables the birds to fly through to the feeder but keeps the squirrels out.

These can work quite well, but there are a few complications. If there is a tray at the bottom of the feeder, then the squirrels can just reach in to get the food that gathers there. If the cylinder of mesh is too small in diameter, then the squirrels may be able to reach

A caged tubular feeder

through it to the feeder portals and scoop out seed. Smaller squirrels, such as Red Squirrels, can often just crawl right through the wire mesh. The feeder also can keep larger birds, such as grackles and jays, from getting at the seed, for the mesh is too small for them to get through.

SPRING-LOADED FEEDERS

Some feeders are basically a hopper feeder with a spring-loaded door that can close over the seed openings. The bottom tray is open on one side and has weights or a spring on the other side, such that when a heavy bird or animal gets on the tray, the opening to the seed hopper closes. You can usually adjust the tension so that it closes for the various weights that you are trying to exclude.

A spring-loaded metal feeder

Make sure you do not mount these feeders so close to a tree or other location that squirrels can just reach over and scoop out the seed without landing on the feeder. Sometimes squirrels learn how to reach down to the feeder openings from the roof of the feeder and get at the seed without tripping the mechanism that closes the door. If you have these exceptionally smart squirrels, then you may need to try caged or mechanical feeders.

MECHANICAL DEVICES

There are a few devices that try to mechanically keep squirrels off feeders. One, called the Droll Yankee Flipper, is very popular and has a motor inside that spins the bottom of the feeder where the perch is. It is activated by the weight of the squirrel, but birds are too light to make it run. When the squirrel

The Droll Yankee Flipper spins squirrels off the perch

lands on the perch, the motor spins the perch and the squirrel jumps or is flung off. It does not hurt the squirrels, and after a few attempts they usually give up and do not go near it.

CHANGING FOODS

If your squirrel problems cannot be solved by any of the baffling or feeder devices, you can try changing the foods you offer the birds to ones that squirrels do not like as much.

There are certain foods squirrels really love, others they like less, and a few they do not like at all. Among their favorites is sunflower seed in all its various forms. They also like corn and nuts of all kinds. Since sunflower is the number-one choice at feeders of the greatest variety of birds, there is a conflict here between the squirrels and the birds.

Try feeding birds safflower instead of sunflower. Some squirrels are not as attracted to this as they are to sunflower. Although birds often like sunflower better, they can get used to safflower. Cardinals seem to accept safflower quite readily. Some people initially mix the safflower with sunflower to get the birds to try it.

Another seed you can offer is Nyjer (thistle). Generally, squirrels do not like it. But all of our finches and many of the smaller birds, such as chickadees and titmice, will eat it.

When you put out suet and it attracts squirrels, it is generally the seeds and other additives they are after. Switching to plain white suet cakes with no seeds or other ingredients mixed in sometimes makes the squirrels less interested, and they may stop going to it altogether. You can also hang suet from poles that are equipped with squirrel baffles.

To summarize: If you have the space, the best plan is to put feeders on a pole in the open with a stovepipe or cone-shaped baffle around the pole. If you do not have the space, then using vari-ous models of squirrel-proof feeders is the next best step. Also, you can try offering foods that are less attractive to squirrels. There is one other thing you can do, and that is to set up separate squirrel feeders to divert the squirrels from the bird feeders.

Yet another approach is to offer squirrels some of their favorite foods in feeders designed just for them. This is nice for people who love to watch squirrels, and for those of you who want to get rid of squirrels, it can distract the squirrels and take the pressure off your regular bird feeders.

CORNCOBS

Squirrels love to eat hard corn off the cob, and you can usually buy cob corn at your local bird supply store. There are many kinds of cob corn feeders. Some are as simple as a spiral of wire into which the cob corn can be placed and then hung off a branch. Others look like a little platform having a metal post onto which you can slide the corn. The squirrel sits behind the

Cob corn in a spring holder

A squirrel chair with cob corn

cob corn to eat it, which can be fun to watch. There are a variety of more elaborate feeders that have little chairs where the squirrel sits.

MUNCH BOXES

There is also a squirrel feeder that is a small box with a clear Plexiglas front and a lid. It can be attached to a tree. You can fill the box with a squirrel food mix, peanuts, or other foods squirrels

A squirrel munch box: the squirrels can sit on the platform and open the lid

like. The squirrel learns to open the top of the box to get the food and then sits on a front platform nibbling away at it. This is also fun to watch.

In many cases, birds spill bits of seed from feeders as they eat and these can keep the squirrels busy below the feeders as they look for tidbits. Do not worry about these squirrels; they may momentarily scare away a few ground birds, but all of the other birds will keep feeding without disturbance.

A Red Squirrel eating fallen seed

Solving Feeder Problems

1. How can I keep squirrels off my feeders?
2. Why are there no birds at my feeders?
3. How can I stop birds from crashing into my windows?
4. A bird keeps pecking at my window. What is it doing, and how can I stop it?
5. How can I keep blackbirds from taking over my feeders?
6. How do I discourage pigeons from coming to my feeders?
7. Why are woodpeckers pecking holes into our house, and how can I stop them?
8. How can I protect my feeder birds from cats?
9. How do I stop birdseed from sprouting under my feeder?
10. How do I protect my feeder birds from hawks?

1. How can I keep squirrels off my feeders?

Squirrels can be real pests at bird feeders, but there are a number of ways you can keep them off and reserve the seed for the birds. For a complete discussion of squirrels, see the Squirrel-Proofing chapter, page 49. Here is a summary of steps you can take.

♦ Place feeders at least 12 feet from any surface the squirrel can jump from, such as a tree, shrub, or house.

♦ If your feeder is pole mounted, put it at least 5 feet off the ground and place a stovepipe or cone baffle below the feeder.

♦ If your feeder is hung from a tree, make sure it is at least 12 feet from the trunk and 5 feet off the ground,

Gray Squirrels can be kept off your feeders in a variety of ways

and place a large dome baffle above the feeder. Some people string a wire between two trees and hang the feeder from the wire; again, make sure it is at least 12 feet away from tree trunks and 5 feet off the ground, and hang a dome baffle above it.

◆ New squirrel-proof feeders are being introduced all the time. Try them and see which works for you. Some tubular feeders now come enclosed in a wire mesh cage. Other feeders are metal boxes with a spring-weighted platform. When a heavy squirrel lands on the platform, a door closes over the feeding holes. Lighter birds can land and feed without the door closing.

◆ Some people like to divert squirrels from feeders by providing them with their own food at an area away from the bird feeders.

2. Why are there no birds at my feeders?

There are many reasons why birds may not visit feeders at a given time. Here are some of the reasons and some things you can do. Some of these topics are described in more detail in other sections of this guide.

◆ **You just started feeding birds:** It can take a while for birds to find and use a new feeder setup. Give them several weeks and be sure that your feeders are placed near where you have seen birds on your property.

◆ **You have poor bird habitat:** If you have few trees or shrubs, birds may not be attracted to your yard. The key to attracting birds is to provide a bird-friendly habitat. Diversity is the most important concept in such a habitat. Provide deciduous and coniferous trees, fruiting shrubs, flowers and vines, grassy areas and weedy areas.

◆ **You do not have a good basic feeder setup:** See the chapter called Five Steps to Bird-Feeding Success to be sure you have the basic feeder setup. This consists of a tubular feeder with sunflower, a tubular feeder with thistle (Nyjer) or finch mix, a hopper or tray feeder with mixed seed, suet, and a birdbath. Also, try putting some seed mix in a tray on the ground; it can attract doves, sparrows, and cardinals, which often prefer to eat off the ground. Use fresh seed and put out only what the birds will eat promptly. Keep all feeders and the area under them clean and remove any moldy seed.

◆ **It is late summer or early fall:** Many birds do not come to feeders as much in late summer and early fall because

This goldfinch is eating some of the abundant fall seeds

this is when there is the most food available to them in the wild. All of the seeds and fruits are maturing, and insects are at their most plentiful. As this food gets eaten and as the weather starts to turn cold, your feeder birds will return.

◆ **Your seed is not fresh:** It is important to keep fresh seed in your feeders, for this is what the birds prefer. If it is old or moldy, the birds may not eat it. To keep seed fresh, store it in a cool dry place in a tight-lidded container. You might try buying seed in smaller quantities to ensure its freshness.

◆ **Squirrels are monopolizing your feeders:** If you have lots of squirrels on your feeders all of the time, then they may keep the birds away. See pages 49–57 for ways to cope with your squirrel problem.

3. How can I stop birds from crashing into my windows?

Birds see the sky reflected in your windows, especially large windows, and think they can fly into it. If they actually hit the glass, they can be stunned or killed. Resident birds on your property can become used to the location of windows and generally avoid them. But young birds, birds on migration that are new to the area, and birds that are suddenly frightened by a hawk, for instance, are more likely to hit windows. Here are some suggestions for reducing this occurrence.

- It is best to move feeders away from the house and away from large windows.
- Put screening over the windows by tacking it to the outside of each window.

- Put bird mesh, the material that garden stores sell to keep birds off berry bushes, etc., over the windows.
- Hang long reflective mylar streamers in front of all the windows. We have found that black plastic silhouettes of hawks, which are sometimes recommended for this purpose, do not work very well for us.

4. A bird keeps pecking at my window. What is it doing, and how can I stop it?

Birds, especially males, can become quite territorial during the breeding season. When they see their reflection in a window or car mirror, they think it is another bird. When they peck at it to make it go away, it seems to peck back, which makes the bird even more aggressive. Generally, after the breeding season the behavior will wane.

To stop this behavior, you need to get rid of the reflection on the outside of the window. Here are some things people have tried:

- Put up screening.
- Cover the window with newspaper.
- Use Bon Ami to make the glass cloudy.
- Cover the window with cloth.

You need to go outside and check your solution from the bird's point of view; make sure you have gotten rid of the reflection on the outside of the window where the bird visits.

5. How can I keep blackbirds from taking over my feeders?

Many people group together all medium-sized blackish birds under the term "blackbird." There are actually several birds that fit in this category: Red-winged Blackbird, Common

Some people try to keep grackles off their feeders

Grackle, Brown-headed Cowbird, and European Starling. You can look up these birds in the Identification Pages.

All of these birds can come to feeders. Grackles and Red-winged Blackbirds are especially likely during migration in spring and fall and eat most kinds of birdseed, so the way to exclude them is through feeders they cannot access. Here are some solutions:

- Use thistle seed (Nyjer) in a thistle tube with tiny holes; it is hard for these larger birds to get their bills through the tiny holes.

- Use sunflower in tube feeders and remove the perches; small birds can still cling to the portals.

- Use a small globe-shaped feeder with small holes at the bottom that only small birds, such as chickadees, can cling to as they feed.

A globe sunflower feeder that only small birds can hold on to

- Use a tube feeder enclosed in a wire cage that lets finches and chickadees enter but excludes larger birds that cannot fit through the openings in the wire.

- Try placing suet cakes in a suet holder that is encased with a similar cage or try an upside-down suet feeder.

- Try safflower seed in a tube. Grackles generally will not eat it.

6. How do I discourage pigeons from coming to my feeders?

If you want to discourage pigeons, first make sure no seed gets on the ground, for that is where pigeons prefer to feed. Also, do not use feeders with wide ledges that enable pigeons to land.

In addition, you should stop feeding any seed that the pigeons like and can access. Use thistle/Nyjer in thistle feeders, for the pigeons generally cannot get at it. However, if too much seed is spilled on the ground by the goldfinches, the pigeons may be attracted. Use suet (pure suet cake without seeds in it) in a suet holder surrounded by a cage that only lets small birds enter. Use hummingbird feeders in season. Try tube feeders with a cage around them or hopper feeders with a spring-loaded opening (see pages 52–53).

If all else fails, stop all feeding except for the hummingbird feeders, birdbaths, and suet. When the pigeons leave, try a few feeders again.

7. Why are woodpeckers pecking holes into our house, and how can I stop them?

Woodpeckers peck for several reasons: to find food, excavate a nest hole, or communicate through extended drumming. Here are some solutions for dealing with woodpeckers that are pecking holes in your house.

- Tie helium balloons on string so they float near the area.
- Put up a plastic decoy owl (sold in garden centers).
- Tack up or drape rubber snakes on the gutter, or near the area of the house where the woodpeckers are excavating.
- Cover the area with screening or hang a piece of half-inch hardware cloth over the area about a half inch out from the surface.

People often have woodpeckers drumming or pecking on their houses

- Tack up a piece of plastic drop cloth a few inches out from the siding. The smooth and slippery surface will keep the woodpecker from landing on the side of the house.

- Hang bird mesh (the kind that gardeners use to keep birds off their blueberries), also out from the siding.

The loud volleys of drumming by woodpeckers on resonant surfaces of your house do not actually excavate wood. They are a communication between mates or neighboring woodpeckers and occur mostly during breeding.

8. How can I protect my feeder birds from cats?

Cats are known to kill millions of birds every year. If you own a cat, keep it indoors. Cats live longer, healthier, and happier lives if they are kept indoors. If you know it is your neighbors' cat, talk to them and encourage them to keep it indoors. The American Bird Conservancy has a program called "Cats Indoors: The Campaign for Safer Birds and Cats." More information on this is available at their website: www.abcbirds.org. If there are neighborhood cats you cannot control, here are some ways to help protect the birds.

- Keep all feeders a good distance from any shrubs or cover where cats could hide.

- Mount feeders on poles with baffles and put a large-diameter circle (15 feet) of fencing around the feeders. We have successfully prevented cats from getting to our feeders by using chicken wire (which is hard for cats to climb) that is 3½ feet high attached to green metal garden poles. Birds can fly into the enclosure, but it is hard for the cat to climb or jump over the fence. Even if a cat does make it over the fence, it is slowed down and the birds have time to flee.

9. How do I stop birdseed from sprouting under my feeder?

The bird-feeding industry is constantly trying to figure out a way to cost-effectively eliminate the sprouting of seeds that fall from feeders onto the ground. The Nyjer industry heat-sterilizes its seed in a commercial process that prevents most seeds from germinating. However, it is very expensive to do and is not currently feasible for all types of seeds.

One solution is to regularly rake up any old seeds, hulls, and debris before seeds have a chance to sprout. Also rake up any seeds that have sprouted. Put feeders in an area clear of grass with bark mulch below. It is easy to rake up the seeds and hulls with the bark mulch and then put down fresh mulch. If you want to keep an area tidy, you can feed sunflower chips, which rarely sprout because they are already broken up and the shell is removed; also, birds love this seed and generally consume all of it. You can also use a no-waste mix that birds tend to entirely consume.

You can also keep seed off the ground by using trays on the bottom of tube feeders or using tray feeders where the seed just remains on the platform.

10. How do I protect my feeder birds from hawks?

There are certain hawks that feed on birds, and they will be attracted to any concentration of small birds. These hawks are collectively called accipiters. The most common at feeders are Sharp-shinned Hawks and Cooper's Hawks. These hawks are not new to feeder birds; small birds have to be on the alert for attacks from them in the wild all the time. If your feeder birds see the hawk first, then they most likely will be able to avoid it. If feeders are placed well away from trees, then the feeder birds can see the hawks coming. You can also help your feeder birds by having brushy areas or brush piles near the feeders so they can dive into them for cover.

If hawks get a bird at your feeder, it is not a reason for stopping feeding.

It is just a close-up example of what is happening in the wild all the time. Once a hawk strikes, the birds become wary and the hawk loses its advantage and usually leaves.

Sharp-shinned Hawks may visit feeders to eat the feeder birds

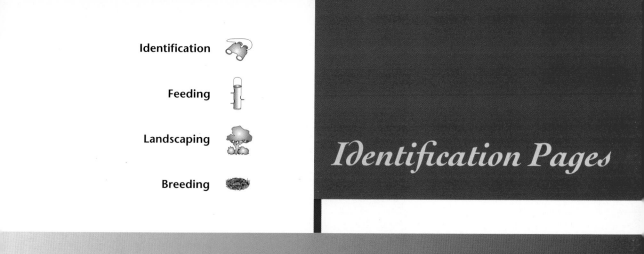

Identification

Feeding

Landscaping

Breeding

Identification Pages

California Quail
Callipepla californica 10"

Identification: Both sexes have a black plume on forehead and scaled appearance on belly. Male has black chin and light forehead; female has a light chin.

Feeding: Feeds on the ground or comes to tray feeders. Prefers cracked corn, millet, seed mixes. Also eats canary seed, milo, oats, black oil sunflower.

Landscaping: These quails like open woods, also fields with brushy patches.

Breeding: Nests on ground near log, rock, or stump, or low in a tree. Eggs: 12–16, creamy white with dark marks; I: 18–23 days; F: 10 days; B: 1–2.

Male

Fun Facts In fall, family groups band together into large flocks, called coveys. These consist of 30 or more birds, sometimes as many as several hundred.

Rock Dove
(Pigeon)
Columba livia 13"

Identification: Dark gray head; iridescent neck; light gray back; 2 dark wing bars. Due to breeding by humans, may be a variety of other colors. Note squared tail and white rump in flight.

Feeding: Feeds on the ground or comes to tray feeders. Enjoys cracked corn, all types of sunflower, seed mixes. Also eats safflower, millet, milo, peanuts, thistle.

Landscaping: Pigeons should not be encouraged to nest. They can dominate feeders and become a nuisance.

Breeding: Nests on ledges on buildings, under bridges, or in barns. Eggs: 1–2, white; I: 18 days; F: 25–29 days; B: 2–5.

Fun Facts Not a native N. American bird, but was introduced by early settlers in the 1600s. Humans have been domesticating pigeons for several thousand years.

71

Mourning Dove
Zenaida macroura 12"

 Identification: Sleek, gray-brown, pigeon-like bird with a long pointed tail and large black spots on wings. Males have iridescence on sides of neck; females lack this. Call is a series of plaintive hoots, with second note higher, "hoo-ah hoo hoo hoo."

Feeding: Feeds on the ground or in a tray feeder. Prefers cracked corn, black oil and hulled sunflower, seed mixes, millet, canary seed. Also eats safflower, striped sunflower, whole corn, hulled peanuts, milo, oats.

 Landscaping: Mourning Doves like to feed on seeds in open areas with little vegetation. They nest in trees.

Breeding: Nests on horizontal branch of tree. Eggs: 2, white; I: 14–15 days; F: 12–14 days; B: 2–4.

Fun Facts Has longest breeding season and most broods of any N. American bird; may nest year-round in southern areas.

Ruby-throated Hummingbird
Archilochus colubris 3½"

 Identification: Male has green upperparts, iridescent red throat, white breast and belly. Female is similar but has a white throat and white spots at corners of tail.

 Feeding: Comes to hummingbird feeders. Consumes sugar water and nectar from plants.

 Landscaping: Plant red tubular flowers for hummingbird nectaring and have a mix of trees and open areas.

Male

Fun Facts In territorial defense, a bird will do a "pendulum display," flying back and forth as though being swung from a string.

 Breeding: Nests on horizontal branch. Eggs: 2, white; I: 16 days; F: 30 days; B: 1–2.

Black-chinned Hummingbird
Archilochus alexandri 3½"

 Identification: Tiny, with greenish upperparts and flanks, whitish underparts. Male has black chin with lower portion violet and white collar; female has plain whitish throat.

 Feeding: Comes to hummingbird feeders. Consumes sugar water and nectar from plants.

 Landscaping: Nests in dry lowlands and foothills; uses fibers from willows and sycamores to build nest.

 Breeding: Builds nest on horizontal branch of tree. Eggs: 2, white; I: 13–16 days; F: 21 days; B: 1–2.

Male

Fun Facts Unlike other hummingbirds, typically does not coat nest with lichens. New nest may be built on top of previous year's.

Anna's Hummingbird
Calypte anna 4"

 Identification: Green upperparts, pale underparts scaled with green. Male has bright rosy iridescence on throat and crown; female has pale throat with patch of red spots in center.

 Feeding: Comes to hummingbird feeders. Consumes sugar water and nectar from plants.

 Landscaping: Anna's Hummingbirds like open areas near gardens with a few trees.

 Breeding: Nests on horizontal branch or on human structure. Eggs: 2, white; I: 14–19 days; F: 18–23 days; B: 1–2.

Male

Fun Facts Exceptionally early breeder; nesting may start in Dec. Male courtship display can involve a speedy dive from 120-foot height.

Acorn Woodpecker
Melanerpes formicivorus 9"

 Identification: Solid black back, red on crown, white eye surrounded by black, white forehead and cheek. Shows white rump and wing patch in flight. Female has wide black border between white forehead and red crown; male's entire crown is red. Gives harsh "rack-up" call.

 Feeding: Comes to tray, ranch, or tube feeders and suet holders. Prefers suet, all types of sunflower, peanut butter, hulled peanuts. Also eats dried fruit, sugar water from hummingbird feeders.

 Landscaping: Plant or encourage existing oaks for acorns and leave dead trees, since these woodpeckers store acorns there.

 Breeding: Excavates nest cavity in tree. Eggs: 4–6, white; I: 14 days; F: 30–32 days; B: 2–3.

Female

Fun Facts Named for its habit of storing acorns in holes that it drills in tree trunks or utility poles. Hundreds of acorns may be stored in a single trunk or pole.

Red-bellied Woodpecker
Melanerpes carolinus 9"

 Identification: Upperparts finely barred black and white; head and underparts light tan. Male has red patch from back of neck to base of bill. Female has red only on back of head.

 Feeding: Comes to tube and tray feeders or suet cages. Prefers suet, all types of sunflower, fresh or dried fruit, and peanut butter. Also eats safflower, seed mixes, hulled peanuts, cracked corn, milo.

 Landscaping: Leave standing dead trees in which the birds can excavate their nest holes.

 Breeding: Excavates nest hole in live tree or uses birdhouse. Eggs: 3–8, white; I: 12–14 days; F: 25–30 days; B: 2–3.

Male

Fun Facts The woodpecker has a long tongue with a barb at the tip. This enables it to reach into crevices and snare insects.

Downy Woodpecker
Picoides pubescens 6"

 Identification: Small, with white underparts, black-and-white-striped head, and black wings with white spots. Male has a red patch on the back of the head; female does not. Gives a high "pick" call and a whinny.

 Feeding: Comes to suet cages and tube feeders. Prefers suet, peanut butter, hulled sunflower. Also eats black oil and striped sunflower, hulled and whole peanuts, seed mixes, safflower, cracked corn.

 Landscaping: Downy Woodpeckers need dead wood in which to excavate their nest cavity, and they also feed off the insects in the bark of the same dead trees. Leave dead trees standing.

 Breeding: Excavates nest hole in dead wood. Eggs: 4–5, white; I: 12 days; F: 21 days; B: 1–2.

Male

Fun Facts In winter, has a roost hole in a tree or a nest box to which it returns each night.

Hairy Woodpecker
Picoides villosus 9"

 Identification: Black wings with white spots; white back and underparts; black-and-white-striped head. Male has red patch on back of head; female does not. Bill is almost as long as head. Gives sharp, high-pitched "teek" call and a short rattle.

 Feeding: Comes to suet cages and tube feeders. Prefers suet, peanut butter, hulled and black oil sunflower, hulled peanuts. Also eats whole peanuts, mixed seed, cracked corn, safflower.

Landscaping: Hairy Woodpeckers need fairly large trees in which to feed and excavate their nest cavity. They can excavate in either living or dead trees.

 Breeding: Excavates nest hole in live trees or dead wood. Eggs: 4–6, white; I: 11–12 days; F: 28–30 days; B: 1.

Male

| *Fun Facts* | Pairs stay together year-round. In threat display, birds sway side to side to defend feeding territory. May drink from hummingbird feeders. |

Northern Flicker
Colaptes auratus 13"

Male

Identification: Brown-and-black-barred back and wings; wide black necklace; whitish or buffy breast with black spots; white rump. "Yellow-shafted" has yellow undertail and under-wings; male has black mustache. "Red-shafted" has red undertail and underwings; male has red mustache.

Feeding: Comes to tube, tray, and ranch feeders, or suet holders on tree trunks. Prefers suet, peanuts, hulled sunflower. Also eats black oil or striped sunflower, seed mixes, cracked corn, peanut butter, dried fruit.

Fun Facts | Unusual for a woodpecker in that it spends much of its time on the ground, probing with its bill into anthills to eat the ants.

Landscaping: Flickers need large dead trees in which to excavate their cavity nests. They feed on lawns as well.

Breeding: Builds nest hole in tree, post, or cactus. May use nest box. Eggs: 7–9, white; I: 11–12 days; F: 14–21 days; B: 1–2.

Steller's Jay
Cyanocitta stelleri 13"

Identification: Long crest; blackish head, breast, and back; sky-blue wings, belly, and tail. Variable amounts of white streaking on face. Gives repeated "shaack shaack" calls.

Feeding: Feeds on the ground, comes to tray or ranch feeders. Likes black oil or striped sunflower, peanuts, peanut butter, seed mixes, cracked corn, suet. Also eats hulled sunflower, milo, millet, fruit.

Landscaping: These jays prefer to live and nest in a variety of evergreen trees or shrubs.

Breeding: Nests in shrub or tree. Eggs: 2–6, blue or pale green marked with brown; I: 16 days; F: 18 days; B: 1.

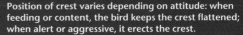

Fun Facts Position of crest varies depending on attitude: when feeding or content, the bird keeps the crest flattened; when alert or aggressive, it erects the crest.

Blue Jay
Cyanocitta cristata 12"

 Identification: Blue above and gray below, with a prominent crest and black collar. Wings and tail are spotted with white. Calls are a harsh "thief thief" and a liquid "toolool." Can also imitate hawks.

 Feeding: Feeds on the ground, at tube, tray, or ranch feeders, and at suet cages. Likes black oil sunflower, seed mixes, striped sunflower, hulled or unshelled peanuts, cracked or whole corn. Also eats hulled sunflower, suet, millet, canary seed, safflower, milo, wheat, peanut butter.

Fun Facts | May imitate the calls of hawks; the reason for this is unknown. Very social and seemingly "smart" birds.

 Landscaping: Jays eat a lot of acorns in the wild, so plant some oaks to attract them.

Breeding: Nests in trees. Eggs: 4–5, greenish blue and spotted with brown; I: 17 days; F: 17–19 days; B: 1–2.

Western Scrub-Jay
Aphelocoma californica   12"

Identification: Slim and long-tailed, with no crest. Blue head, wings, and tail; gray back; white eyebrow; white throat streaked with grayish.

Feeding: Comes to tray or ranch feeders, feeds on the ground. Enjoys peanuts, seed mixes, cracked corn, striped or black oil sunflower, peanut butter, suet. Also eats hulled sunflower, millet, milo.

Landscaping: Plant oak trees, for this jay loves to eat acorns.

Breeding: Nests in shrubs. Eggs: 2–6, pale green or gray with reddish-brown marks; I: 16–19 days; F: 18 days; B: 1–2.

Fun Facts | Like other members of the crow and jay family, scrub-jays often cache food, hiding it in several locations for later feeding. In feeding flocks, one bird may act as "lookout."

83

Black-billed Magpie
Pica pica 20"

Identification: Large and striking with very long tail. Head, breast, and back black; wings and tail iridescent bluish; white belly and wing patch. Common call is an inquisitive "ahg?"

Feeding: Comes to hanging or hopper feeders; feeds on the ground. Prefers peanuts, peanut butter mixes, and suet. Also eats millet, cracked corn, black oil or striped sunflower, whole corn, fresh fruit, milo.

Landscaping: This adaptable bird can nest in a wide variety of areas with mixed trees and shrubs.

Breeding: Nests in tree or shrub, sometimes in colonies. Eggs: 2–9, blue-green with brown speckles; I: 14–23 days; F: 10 days; B: 1.

Fun Facts Eats carrion, sometimes following predators until they make a kill; may also land on large animals and eat insect pests off them.

American Crow
Corvus brachyrhynchos 18"

 Identification: Very familiar; large, all-black bird with a large black bill. Gives "caw" notes with some variations.

 Feeding: Feeds on the ground or in tray feeders. Likes whole or hulled peanuts, cracked corn, whole corn, peanut butter, suet. Also eats seed mixes, all types of sunflower, fresh or dried fruit, millet, milo.

 Fun Facts On fall and winter nights, hundreds to tens of thousands of crows roost together in trees. These communal roosts may be in cities or forests; some birds may fly 50 miles to join the roost.

 Landscaping: Crows like partially open areas and often nest in the tops of tall evergreens, where their nest is hidden.

 Breeding: Nests in trees. Eggs: 4–5, bluish green with brown marks; I: 18 days; F: 28–35 days; B: 1–2.

Black-capped Chickadee

Poecile atricapillus 5"

 Identification: Black cap and bib; white cheek; gray back; variably buffy on flanks. Sings two whistled notes, the first one higher, like "fee-bee." Also gives "chickadeedee" call.

Feeding: Prefers seed and suet provided in hanging feeders. Favorite foods are suet; striped, black oil, and hulled sunflower; hulled peanuts; peanut butter. Also eats safflower, seed mixes, millet, cracked corn, canary seed, milo, oats.

Fun Facts — Territorial breeding pairs join small winter flocks, which have a complex social structure. A flock defends a winter feeding territory of about 20 acres from other chickadees.

 Landscaping: Chickadees need nest boxes or dead trees in which they can excavate for their nests. Leave some dead trees standing for them.

 Breeding: Nests in tree cavity or birdhouse. Eggs: 6–8, white with speckles; I: 11–12 days; F: 15–17 days; B: 1–2.

Carolina Chickadee
Poecile carolinensis 5"

Identification: Small with black cap and throat, white cheek, gray back, pale underparts, and buffy flanks. Sings a 4-syllable whistled song with 1st and 3rd notes highest: "Fee-bee fee-bay." Gives "chickadeedee" call.

Feeding: Comes to tube feeders and suet holders. Prefers suet, all types of sunflower, hulled peanuts, peanut butter. Also eats seed mixes, safflower, cracked corn, millet, thistle.

Fun Facts Chickadees store food in many different locations for later feeding. They show a remarkable ability to remember each hiding place.

Landscaping: Keeping some dead trees standing will provide food and nesting opportunities for this species.

Breeding: Excavates nest hole in dead tree or uses birdhouse. Eggs: 6–8, white with speckles; I: 11–12 days; F: 13–17 days; B: 1–2.

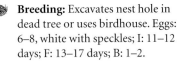

87

Mountain Chickadee
Poecile gambeli 6"

 Identification: Gray overall with black cap and bib, white cheek, and thin white line over eye. In summer, white eyebrow may be worn away as bird goes in and out of nest hole. Sings 3–4 whistled notes, like "feebee feebee." Gives raspy "chickadeedeedee" call.

 Feeding: Comes to tube, tray, or ranch feeders and suet holders. Prefers suet, black oil sunflower, striped sunflower, peanut butter. Also eats hulled sunflower, hulled peanuts, seed mixes, safflower, millet, cracked corn.

Fun Facts Young birds may join foraging flocks of Bushtits (see p. 92).

 Landscaping: Prefers to live in evergreen forests at upper elevations.

 Breeding: Excavates nest cavity or nests in birdhouse. Eggs: 7–9, white; I: 14 days; F: 17–20 days; B: 1–2.

Chestnut-backed Chickadee
Poecile rufescens 5"

Identification: Small with black cap and bib, white cheek, bright reddish-brown back, and gray to reddish flanks. Gives hoarse "chick-dee-dee" call; does not have whistled song.

Feeding: Comes to tube, tray, or ranch feeders and suet holders. Enjoys suet, black oil sunflower, hulled sunflower, peanut butter, hulled peanuts. Also eats striped sunflower, seed mixes, thistle, safflower, millet.

Fun Facts Other birds often follow flocks of chickadees as they search for food; chickadee calls alert these followers to the presence of food or danger.

Landscaping: Will accept birdhouses but prefers to excavate in soft rotted wood.

 Breeding: Excavates tree cavity or nests in birdhouse. Eggs: 6–7, white with reddish speckles; I: 11–12 days; F: 13–17 days; B: 1–2.

Oak Titmouse
Baeolophus inornatus 5½"

Juniper Titmouse
Baeolophus griseus 5½"

 Identification: Small, entirely plain gray, with small crest.

 Feeding: Comes to tube, tray, or ranch feeders and suet holders. Prefers suet, all types of sunflower, peanut butter. Also eats seed mixes, peanuts, safflower, milo, millet.

 Landscaping: Titmice need woods, where they eat tree seeds and nest in natural cavities.

Fun Facts Formerly a single species called Plain Titmouse. Oak Titmouse (shown) lives along Pacific Coast, Juniper Titmouse in interior West.

Breeding: Nests in old woodpecker hole or in birdhouse. Eggs: 6–8, whitish, sometimes with small brown dots; I: 14–16 days; F: 16–21 days; B: 1–2.

Tufted Titmouse
Baeolophus bicolor 5"

 Identification: Small crested bird; gray above; white below with buffy sides. Song is series of downslurred whistles, like "peter peter peter." Gives scolding calls, "jwee jwee jwee."

Feeding: Feeds at tube, tray, or ranch feeders and at suet cages. Likes all types of sunflower, suet, hulled peanuts, peanut butter, safflower. Also eats seed mixes, cracked corn, millet, milo.

Fun Facts Since the 1950s, the titmouse has been expanding its range northward, thanks in part to increased use of bird feeders, which enable the birds to survive the winter.

 Landscaping: Titmice need nest boxes or existing tree cavities in which to nest. They often eat insects off pines.

 Breeding: Nests in tree cavities or birdhouses. Eggs: 4–8, white with small brown dots; I: 13–14 days; F: 17–18 days; B: 1–2.

Bushtit
Psaltriparus minimus 3½"

 Identification: Tiny and gray with long tail and small bill. Coastal birds are paler with a grayish-brown cap; interior birds are darker with a brownish cheek. Male's eyes are dark, female's yellow.

 Feeding: Comes to hanging feeders and suet holders. Likes suet, peanut butter. Also eats black oil sunflower.

 Landscaping: Likes parks and gardens where there are open woods and shrubs.

Fun Facts | Flocks confuse potential predators, such as hawks, by all giving a monotone trill at once, making individual birds hard to locate. Winter flocks may roost huddled together.

 Breeding: Attaches nest to twigs of tree or bush. Eggs: 5–7, white; I: 12 days; F: 14–15 days; B: 1–2.

Red-breasted Nuthatch
Sitta canadensis 4½"

 Identification: Small and compact; black crown, nape, and eyestripe; white cheek and eyebrow; rust-colored breast. Female has gray cap and pale rusty underparts. Gives a nasal "nyeep nyeep nyeep," higher-pitched than White-breasted Nuthatch (see next page).

 Feeding: Comes to tube, tray, and hopper feeders; suet cages. Prefers suet, all types of sunflower, hulled peanuts, peanut butter. Also eats whole peanuts, seed mixes, cracked corn, safflower.

 Fun Facts "Irruptive" species, appearing in large numbers farther south in some winters but absent other winters. A pugnacious little bird that can drive larger species from feeders.

 Landscaping: Needs soft or rotted wood in which to excavate a nest hole, or can use another bird's or existing cavity.

Breeding: Nests in natural cavities or birdhouses. Eggs: 5–7, white or slightly pink with brown spots; I: 12 days; F: 16–21 days; B: 1–2.

White-breasted Nuthatch
Sitta carolinensis 6"

Identification: Small stubby-looking bird. Gray back; black across top of head; white face and underparts. Gives nasal "yank yank" calls.

Feeding: Comes to tube or hopper feeders and suet cages. Prefers suet; hulled, black oil, and striped sunflower; hulled peanuts; peanut butter. Also eats seed mixes, cracked corn, safflower.

Landscaping: Nuthatches need nest boxes or existing tree cavities in which to nest. They like to feed on insects in the rough bark of trees.

Breeding: Nests in natural cavities or birdhouses. Eggs: 3–10, white with dark marks; I: 12 days; F: 14 days; B: 1–2.

Fun Facts — Nuthatches often take food from feeders and store it in bark crevices to be eaten later. These caches may be stolen by other birds, however.

Carolina Wren
Thryothorus ludovicianus 6"

Identification: Small with long bill and short tail. Rich brown above, orange-buff below, with bold white eyebrow. Sings loud, repeated 3-note phrases like "teakettle, teakettle, teakettle, tea."

Feeding: Comes to tube feeders and suet holders. Enjoys hulled peanuts, peanut butter mixes, suet. Also eats all types of sunflower, millet, seed mixes, cracked corn, milo, safflower, fruit.

Fun Facts Range has expanded northward in recent years. Nests and roosts in buildings, potted plants, cans, and even old boots left outside.

Landscaping: Keep shrubby areas and tangles for this bird to nest in. Also create a brush pile as a possible nesting site.

Breeding: Nests in natural cavity, birdhouse, or crevice. Eggs: 4–8, creamy with brown marks; I: 12–14 days; F: 12–14 days; B: 2–3.

Eastern Bluebird
Sialia sialis 6½"

Identification: Male has brilliant blue head, back, wings, and tail; brick-red throat and breast; and white belly. Female has light blue wings and tail; grayish-blue head and back; buffy throat and breast; and white belly.

Feeding: Comes to tray feeders. Prefers mealworms, dried fruit, suet. Also eats seed mixes, striped sunflower, hulled peanuts, peanut butter.

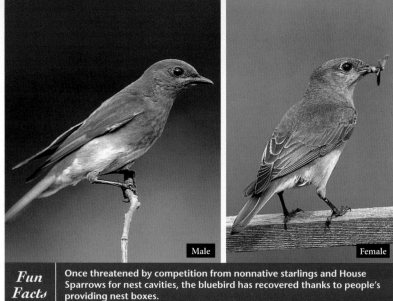

Male

Female

Fun Facts Once threatened by competition from nonnative starlings and House Sparrows for nest cavities, the bluebird has recovered thanks to people's providing nest boxes.

Landscaping: Eastern Bluebirds prefer to feed from perches above areas of lawn, short grass, or sparse vegetation.

Breeding: Nests in natural cavity or birdhouse. Eggs: 3–6, pale blue or white; I: 12–18 days; F: 16–21 days; B: 2–3.

Gray Catbird
Dumetella carolinensis   9"

Identification: All gray with a black cap and reddish-brown patch under base of tail. Song consists of squeaky imitations of other birds' songs, given one at a time. Gives a mewing call.

Feeding: Comes to tray feeders and suet holders. Enjoys suet, grape jelly, hulled sunflower, fruit.

Landscaping: Catbirds nest in dense shrubs at the edge of open areas and love to eat berries of all kinds.

Breeding: Nests in shrub, vine, or small tree. Eggs: 2–6, dark blue-green; I: 12–14 days; F: 10–13 days; B: 1–2.

Fun Facts Named for the fact that its call sounds like the "meow" of a cat. Attempts to imitate a wide variety of natural sounds, but does not do so as well as a mockingbird.

Northern Mockingbird
Mimus polyglottos 11"

Identification: Grayish above and whitish below, with long tail, white patches on wings, and whitish eye. Song consists of imitations of other birds' vocalizations, each one repeated several times.

Feeding: May come to tray feeders or suet holders. Prefers fruit, peanut butter, flavored suet. Also eats seed mixes, all types of sunflower, hulled peanuts.

Landscaping: Mockingbirds are particularly drawn to shrubs and trees with winter berries and will even form a winter territory around them.

Fun Facts: Individuals may be able to imitate up to 200 different birds' calls and other sounds. In summer, mockingbirds may sing all night long.

Breeding: Nests in bushes or small trees. Eggs: 2–6, blue-green with brown marks; I: 12–13 days; F: 10–13 days; B: 1–3.

European Starling
Sturnus vulgaris 8"

Identification: Plump with long pointed bill. In summer, glossy black with yellow bill. In winter, black speckled with white and gold; bill black. Song is a string of squeals, squawks, wolf whistles, and imitations of other birds' calls.

Feeding: Feeds on the ground, at tube, tray, or ranch feeders, and at suet cages. Prefers suet, peanut butter, cracked corn, seed mixes, hulled peanuts. Also eats black oil and hulled sunflower, milo, millet, whole corn, canary seed, wheat, oats.

Landscaping: Starlings should not be encouraged, since they compete with native birds for existing tree cavities.

Breeding: Nests in cavities. Eggs: 2–8, light blue with dark marks; I: 12–14 days; F: 18–21 days; B: 1–3.

Summer plumage

Fun Facts Brought from England and released in Central Park in New York City in 1890, as "props" for Shakespeare plays. Usurps nest cavities from native birds.

Northern Cardinal
Cardinalis cardinalis 8½"

Identification: Male is all red with a crest; black face surrounds reddish bill. Female is buffy below and grayish above, with reddish bill, crest, wings, and tail.

Feeding: Feeds on the ground or on feeders with wide ledges. Prefers striped and black oil sunflower, hulled sunflower, millet, safflower, seed mixes. Also eats whole or cracked corn, canary seed, milo, peanuts.

Landscaping: Plant trees and shrubs that produce seeds or berries, for these are their favorite foods in the wild.

Breeding: Nests in dense shrubbery. Eggs: 2–5, buff-white with dark marks; I: 12–13 days; F: 9–12 days; B: 1–4.

Male

Female

Fun Facts First birds at a feeder before dawn; last to visit after dusk. Both sexes sing, and do so year-round. During courtship, males may feed females at feeders.

Rose-breasted Grosbeak
Pheucticus ludovicianus 8"

Identification: Male has black head, black-and-white upper-parts, and white underparts with a bright red triangle on breast. Female is brown with a bold white eyebrow and streaked white breast. Song is a rapid series of mellow, whistled phrases; call is a loud squeak.

Feeding: Comes to tray, ranch, or tube feeders. Enjoys all types of sunflower, millet, seed mixes, thistle, fresh or dried fruit.

Male

Female

Fun Facts Both sexes sing. Male helps incubate and raise young; he sometimes sings while sitting on the nest.

Landscaping: Nests are generally built in shrubs or small trees at the edge of open areas.

Breeding: Nests in trees. Eggs: 3–6, pale blue with brown spots; I: 12–14 days; F: 9–12 days; B: 1–2.

Eastern Towhee
Pipilo erythrophthalmus 8"

 Identification: Male has black hood and back, orange-brown sides, and white belly. Female resembles male but has brown upperparts.

 Feeding: Feeds on the ground; may come to tray feeders. Prefers millet, seed mixes. Also eats all types of sunflower, cracked corn, milo, canary seed, suet.

Landscaping: Towhees like open woods with a shrub understory.

Breeding: Nests on or near ground in brushy areas. Eggs: 2–6, creamy with brown spots; I: 12–13 days; F: 10–12 days; B: 1–3.

Male

Female

 Fun Facts Feeds by jumping backward and scratching the ground vigorously with both feet, even when food is exposed. Debris can be flung backward a yard or more.

Spotted Towhee
Pipilo maculatus 8"

Male

 Identification: Male has black hood, back, and wings; red eyes; white belly; reddish-orange flanks. Back and wings are heavily spotted with white. Female is brown instead of black. Song is a high trill; also gives mewing "chwee" call.

 Feeding: Usually feeds on the ground; may come to tray feeders. Prefers millet and seed mixes. Also eats all types of sunflower, cracked corn, canary seed, milo.

 Fun Facts — This and the Eastern Towhee (p. 102) were formerly a single species called the Rufous-sided Towhee. Often shy and nervous at feeders.

Landscaping: Towhees like to nest on the ground in open woods with a shrub understory.

Breeding: Nests on the ground or low in shrub. Eggs: 2–6, creamy with brown spots; I: 12–13 days; F: 10–12 days; B: 1–3.

California Towhee
Pipilo crissalis   9"

Identification: Dark grayish-brown overall. Has long tail with reddish-brown patch under base, and buffy throat with "necklace" of short streaks.

Feeding: Feeds on the ground; comes to tray feeders. Prefers millet, seed mixes, milo. Also eats cracked corn, black oil sunflower, dried fruit.

Landscaping: Likes to live along streams with cottonwood and willow trees.

Fun Facts — Curious and bold, these birds readily approach humans at picnic areas or yards in search of food. Mates stay close together all year long.

Breeding: Nests on ground or low in bush. Eggs: 2–6, light blue with dark marks; I: 11 days; F: 8 days; B: 2–3.

American Tree Sparrow
Spizella arborea 6"

 Identification: Reddish-brown crown and eyeline; unstreaked gray underparts with black spot on breast; warm brown wings with two white bars; black-and-yellow bill. Feeding call is a musical "teedle-eet."

 Feeding: Feeds on the ground or comes to tray feeders. Enjoys millet, seed mixes, cracked corn. Also eats canary seed, all types of sunflower, thistle.

 Landscaping: Loves to feed along weedy, brushy edges of open areas.

 Breeding: Nests on ground or in shrub. Eggs: 3–5, pale greenish or bluish white; I: 12–13 days; F: 9–10 days; B: 1.

Fun Facts | Untrue to its name, this sparrow is most easily found in areas of tall weeds or brush.

Chipping Sparrow
Spizella passerina 5½"

 Identification: Small sparrow with clear gray breast, reddish cap, white eyebrow, and thin black eyeline. In winter, has buffy head with brown streaked crown; faint eyeline and cheek patch. Song is a rapid trill on one pitch.

Feeding: Comes to tube, ranch, and tray feeders; also feeds on the ground. Enjoys millet, seed mixes, canary seed, hulled sunflower. Also eats cracked corn, black oil and striped sunflower, thistle, milo.

Fun Facts May be confused with the closely related American Tree Sparrow (p. 105), but the Chipping is more common in summer, the Tree in winter.

 Landscaping: Chipping Sparrows often nest in small evergreen plantings that form the foundation plantings of houses.

 Breeding: Nests in tree or shrub. Eggs: 3–4, pale blue with dark blotches; I: 11–12 days; F: 7–10 days; B: 2.

Fox Sparrow
Passerella iliaca 7"

 Identification: Large sparrow with brown or reddish-brown streaking on gray head and back. Whitish underparts boldly streaked with brown or reddish brown; breast may have central spot. Eastern birds redder, western birds brown or grayish brown.

 Feeding: Feeds on the ground or in tray feeders. Prefers seed mixes, cracked corn, millet, milo. Also eats all types of sunflower, thistle.

Fun Facts In characteristic feeding behavior, jumps up and kicks backward with feet, displacing debris to find food underneath.

 Landscaping: Fox Sparrows like to live and feed in brushy edges of woods.

 Breeding: Nests on the ground under trees or shrubs. Eggs: 4–6, light blue-green with dark marks; I: 11–14 days; F: 7–12 days; B: 1–2.

107

Song Sparrow
Melospiza melodia   6"

Identification: Brown-streaked whitish breast has dark central spot; long rounded tail; gray eyebrow; heavy brown stripes off base of bill.

Feeding: Feeds on the ground, or comes to tray and hopper feeders. Likes millet, seed mixes. Also eats safflower, all types of sunflower, thistle, cracked corn, milo, canary seed.

Fun Facts   An exceptionally adaptable bird that lives in a wide variety of habitats. Its song is one of the prettiest in spring.

Landscaping: Create hedgerows and clusters of shrubs in open areas for this sparrow to nest in.

Breeding: Nests on ground or in shrub. Eggs: 3–5, greenish white with dark marks; I: 12–13 days; F: 10 days; B: 2–3.

White-throated Sparrow
Zonotrichia albicollis 6½"

White morph with white eyebrow

Tan morph with tan eyebrow

Identification: Two dark crown stripes; light eyebrow with yellow spot near bill; white throat; clear gray breast. There are two forms: one has a white eyebrow, and the other has a buffy eyebrow.

Feeding: Feeds mainly on the ground or in tray feeders. Prefers seed mixes, millet. Also eats all types of sunflower, canary seed, cracked corn, safflower, milo.

Landscaping: Generally lives in coniferous woods that have openings with brushy areas. Nests on the ground under a small shrub or tree.

Fun Facts In flocks at feeders, may sing a high, whistled song with first note lower, like "old Sam Peabody, Peabody, Peabody." Birds are attracted to imitations of their song.

Breeding: Nests on the ground under a bush or small tree. Eggs: 4–6, light blue-green with dark marks; I: 11–14 days; F: 7–12 days; B: 1–2.

Golden-crowned Sparrow
Zonotrichia atricapilla 7"

Identification: Large sparrow with black crown that has yellow center; gray face and underparts; white eye-ring. Immatures have brown crown with yellow at the front, brownish face and underparts.

Feeding: Feeds on the ground or comes to tray feeders. Prefers millet, seed mixes, cracked corn, milo. Also eats black oil sunflower, peanut butter, thistle, suet, canary seed, striped or hulled sunflower.

Fun Facts | A familiar bird to nineteenth-century gold miners, though not a popular one, since its plaintive whistled song sounds like "no gold here."

Landscaping: This sparrow prefers to nest on the ground near areas with dense shrubs or thickets.

Breeding: Usually nests on ground. Eggs: 3–5, creamy or light blue; I: ?; F: ?; B: 1 or more.

White-crowned Sparrow
Zonotrichia leucophrys 7"

Fun Facts: Dominance within a flock is determined by brightness of plumage; brightest birds are dominant. In experiments, dull-colored birds painted brighter became more dominant.

Identification: Large sparrow with black-and-white-striped head; pink-orange bill; gray nape, face, and breast. Immature has pale brown and reddish-brown striped head.

Feeding: Feeds on the ground or comes to tray feeders. Prefers millet, seed mixes, cracked corn, milo. Also eats hulled peanuts, all types of sunflower, thistle, safflower.

Landscaping: Create a varied habitat of shrubs and open spaces.

Breeding: Nests on the ground or in shrub. Eggs: 3–5, pale blue or green with dark spots; I: 11–15 days; F: 10 days; B: 1–4.

Dark-eyed Junco
Junco hyemalis 6"

Identification: Dark gray (male) to brownish-gray (female) with a white belly, pale pink bill, and white tail edges. Call is a short "tsick"; song is a chiming trill.

Feeding: Prefers seed scattered on the ground or in trays. Likes seed mixes, hulled sunflower, millet, cracked corn. Also eats canary seed, black oil sunflower, and striped sunflower.

Landscaping: Brush piles may be used for cover and roosting.

Breeding: Nest placed in depression in ground near tall vegetation. Eggs: 3–6, gray or pale bluish with dark blotches; I: 12–13 days; F: 9–13 days; B: 1–2.

Slate-colored population most common in the East

Oregon population common in the West

Fun Facts Form flocks which return to the same areas each winter. Certain individuals are dominant within a flock.

Red-winged Blackbird
Agelaius phoeniceus 8½"

 Identification: Male is all black with red shoulder patch that has yellowish border. Female is brown above, heavily streaked brown below, with buffy or whitish eyebrow. Song is a distinctive "oka-*lee*."

Feeding: Feeds on the ground or comes to tray feeders. Likes millet, seed mixes, striped sunflower, cracked corn. Also eats hulled sunflower, safflower, black oil sunflower, hulled peanuts, whole corn.

Male

Female

Fun Facts In winter, birds roost together at night in sometimes spectacular numbers; a few roosts in the Southeast contain millions of birds.

 Landscaping: Prefers wet marshy areas with cattails, but may also live and breed in meadows.

 Breeding: Nests in marsh, among tall grasses or in shrub. Eggs: 3–5, pale greenish blue with dark marks; I: 11 days; F: 11 days; B: 2–3.

113

Common Grackle
Quiscalus quiscula   12"

 Identification: Black with glossy iridescence on head, back, and belly; yellow eye. Female resembles male but has shorter tail and less iridescence. Calls are harsh and grating; song is an upslurred squeak, like "grideleeek."

 Feeding: Feeds on the ground, at tube, tray, or ranch feeders, and at suet cages. Prefers seed mixes, all types of sunflower, cracked corn. Also eats hulled peanuts, suet, peanut butter, millet, milo.

Fun Facts | In aggressive display, birds point their bills skyward as they face each other. This can be seen as they compete at feeders.

Landscaping: Grackles like to nest in dense evergreen trees in somewhat open areas.

 Breeding: Nests in shrubs or trees, usually near ground. Eggs: 4–7, pale greenish brown with dark marks; I: 13–14 days; F: 12–16 days; B: 1.

Brown-headed Cowbird
Molothrus ater 7"

Identification: Male is glossy black with a brown head and dark gray conical bill. Female is grayish brown overall with some faint streaking on breast.

Feeding: Comes to a variety of feeders, and feeds on the ground. Favors mixed seed, millet, cracked corn, pet food. Also eats black oil, striped, and hulled sunflower; safflower; hulled peanuts; suet; bird puddings; canary seed; milo; dried fruit; oats.

Male

Female

Fun Facts Young cowbirds grow up in other birds' nests, but can still recognize their own species when mating.

Landscaping: This bird should not be encouraged, since it parasitizes our other nesting birds.

Breeding: Nest parasite: does not nest, but lays egg in nest of smaller bird. Eggs: 1, sometimes 2, per host nest, white with dark marks; I: 10–13 days; F: 9–11 days; B: ?

Baltimore Oriole
Icterus galbula 8½"

 Identification: Male has black hood, back, and wings; orange body. Females are orange-yellow; head and back mottled with black. Song is 4–8 clear, whistled notes; also gives a rapid chatter.

Feeding: Comes to oriole nectar feeders, tray feeders, or suet holders. Enjoys sugar water, oranges, mealworms, flavored suet, dried fruit.

 Landscaping: Baltimore Orioles like to build nests from the tips of tree branches that hang over open areas.

Male

Female

Fun Facts Orioles will take short pieces of yarn put out for them and weave them into their nests. Older females may acquire a dark head, much like the males.

 Breeding: Hangs nest from tree branch. Eggs: 4–6, pale bluish and white with dark marks; I: 12–14 days; F: 12–14 days; B: 1.

Bullock's Oriole
Icterus bullockii 8½"

 Identification: Male is bright orange with black back, eyeline, and throat; large white wing patch. Female has yellowish head, breast, and undertail; two pale wing bars.

 Feeding: Comes to oriole nectar feeders, tray feeders, or suet holders. Eats sugar water, oranges, flavored suet, mealworms, dried fruit.

 Landscaping: Nests in a variety of trees growing out over open lawns, roads, and streams.

 Breeding: Builds hanging nest on tree branch. Eggs: 4–6, pale bluish white with dark marks; I: 12–14 days; F: 12–14 days; B: 1.

Male

Female

Fun Facts — Formerly this and the Baltimore Oriole were considered a single species called the Northern Oriole. Often drinks nectar from flowers.

Purple Finch
Carpodacus purpureus   6"

 Identification: In male, head, upperparts, breast, and sides are raspberry red; little or no brown streaking on flanks. Female has boldly patterned head with white eyebrow, brown eyeline, and white cheek stripe; broad brown streaks on white underparts. Song is a lively, variable warble. Call is a flat "pik."

 Feeding: Comes to tube, tray, or hopper feeders. Likes thistle and all types of sunflower. Also eats canary seed, millet, seed mixes, cracked corn, safflower, peanut hearts.

Landscaping: Plant trees that produce seeds or berries for these birds to eat. They also like conifers for nesting.

Male

Female

Fun Facts Numerous in the South during winters when northern cone crop is sparse. Population has declined since introduction of House Sparrow and House Finch.

Breeding: Nests in trees. Eggs: 3–6, light blue-green with dark marks; I: 13 days; F: 14 days; B: 1–2.

118

House Finch
Carpodacus mexicanus 5½"

Identification: Broad brown streaking on breast and belly. Male has red head and upper breast; female has uniformly fine-streaked head. Song is a musical warble ending in a downslurred "jeer."

Feeding: Comes to tube feeders, especially thistle feeders. Prefers thistle, hulled sunflower, and finch seed mix. Also eats black oil sunflower, safflower, and seed mixes.

Male

Female

Fun Facts A western species imported and sold in New York City in the 1940s. They were illegally released and have established a widespread eastern population.

Landscaping: House Finches like to nest in hanging planters around patios.

Breeding: Nests in shrub, vine, or hanging plant. Eggs: 2–6, bluish white with speckles; I: 12–16 days; F: 11–19 days; B: 1–3.

Common Redpoll
Carduelis flammea 5½"

 Identification: Pale overall with red forehead, black face, small bill, and streaked flanks. Male has rosy-red breast; female has plain white breast.

 Feeding: Comes to tube feeders and specialized thistle feeders. Prefers thistle, hulled sunflower, and finch seed mixes. Also eats black oil and striped sunflower, seed mixes, cracked corn, millet.

 Landscaping: Redpolls like to feed on small seeds from trees and shrubs like birch and alder.

Breeding: Nests in a bush or on the ground. Eggs: 4–7, pale green or blue with dark marks; I: 10–11 days; F: 12 days; B: 1–2.

Female

Fun Facts Common in some winters, absent in others. Southward movements occur in years when northern birches and alders produce few seeds.

120

Pine Siskin
Carduelis pinus 5"

Identification: Small brown-streaked bird with sharply pointed bill. Variable amounts of yellow on wings and base of tail. Gives harsh, ascending "zreeeee" call.

Feeding: Comes to tube feeders. Likes thistle, hulled sunflower, and black oil sunflower. Also eats millet, seed mixes, safflower, striped sunflower, canary seed, finch seed mix, cracked corn, milo, peanut hearts, peanut butter.

Landscaping: Add coniferous trees, for Pine Siskins love to nest in them and eat their seeds.

Breeding: Nests in trees. Eggs: 1–5, light blue-green with dark marks; I: 13 days; F: 14–15 days; B: 1–2.

Fun Facts: Occurs irregularly within its winter range. Can be attracted to sources of salt, such as that used on roads in winter.

Lesser Goldfinch
Carduelis psaltria 4½"

Male

Female

Identification: Male has yellow belly, white patch on wings. Western birds have black cap and streaked green back; in eastern half of range, upperparts are entirely black. Female is greenish above, yellow below, with white patch on black wings.

Feeding: Comes to tube feeders and specialized thistle feeders. Prefers thistle and hulled sunflower. Also eats seed mixes, black oil sunflower, and finch mixes.

Fun Facts: Goldfinches tend to sit at feeders and keep eating for a long time; other species often take a seed and fly away to eat it.

Landscaping: Lesser Goldfinches love to eat the seeds from flowers like cosmos and sunflower.

Breeding: Nests in shrub or tree. Eggs: 3–6, bluish white; I: 12 days; F: unknown; B: 1, possibly more.

American Goldfinch
Carduelis tristis 5"

 Identification: In summer, male has bright yellow body with black cap, wings, and tail; female is paler olive-yellow with all-yellow head. Winter birds are grayish brown with little yellow. Gives "perchicoree" call in flight, and has long warbling song.

Feeding: Comes to tube feeders, specialized thistle tube feeders with tiny holes, or thistle socks. Strongly prefers thistle and, to a lesser extent, hulled sunflower. Also eats finch seed mixes, black oil sunflower, millet, striped sunflower, safflower, cracked corn, milo, wheat, hulled peanuts.

Summer female

Winter

Summer male

Fun Facts Begins nesting much later than other birds, starting in July. Adults bring their young to feeders and give them seed in late summer and fall.

Landscaping: Plant lots of flowers in the Composite family, such as cosmos, daisies, sunflowers, for American Goldfinches love to eat the seeds. They nest in small trees or shrubs.

 Breeding: Nest placed in shrub or tree. Eggs: 3–7, light blue; I: 12–14 days; F: 11–15 days; B: 1–2.

123

Evening Grosbeak
Coccothraustes vespertinus 8"

Identification: A large finchlike bird with a massive bill. Male has bright yellow body, dark head with bright yellow eyebrow, and black-and-white wings. Female is similar but brownish gray instead of yellow.

Feeding: Comes to tray or hopper feeders, feeds on the ground. Prefers all types of sunflower and seed mixes. Also eats millet, cracked corn, peanut hearts, canary seed, safflower, milo.

Male

Female

Fun Facts Seeds of box elder, or ash-leaved maple, trees are major food source for Evening Grosbeaks. Flocks travel together in search of food.

Landscaping: Plant trees with winter berries, like mountain ash, or trees with winter seeds, such as ash, for these birds to feed on.

Breeding: Nest is placed at the end of a tree branch. Eggs: 2–5, blue or bluish green with dark marks; I: 11–14 days; F: 13–14 days; B: 2.

House Sparrow
Passer domesticus 6"

Male

Female

 Identification: Male has black bib, gray crown and cheek, chestnut-brown nape and back. Female has grayish-brown breast, brown crown, buffy eyebrow, yellowish bill. Gives an emphatic "chirp" call, sometimes in short series "chirrup chirreep chirrup."

 Fun Facts Brought to New York from England in 1850 to control insect pests; has since become abundant. Takes over nest cavities from native birds.

Feeding: Uses tube, tray, and hopper feeders. Likes black oil and hulled sunflower, seed mixes, cracked corn, millet, milo. Also eats safflower, thistle, canary seed, striped sunflower, hulled peanuts, suet, peanut butter.

 Landscaping: House Sparrows should not be encouraged, since they are aggressive to native hole-nesting species and may even kill them.

Breeding: Uses nest cavities and birdhouses; also nests inside buildings, traffic lights, vents, and crevices in walls. Eggs: 3–7, white or light blue with dark marks; I: 10–14 days; F: 14–17 days; B: 2–3.

Resources

To help you learn more about bird feeding and expand your knowledge of the wonderful and exciting lives of birds, here is a list of some of the best books, magazines, and websites, as well as organizations and clubs that you can join.

BOOKS

Stokes, Donald. *Stokes Guide to Bird Behavior, Volume I.* Boston: Little, Brown, 1979.

Stokes, Donald and Lillian. *Stokes Beginner's Guide to Birds: Eastern Region.* Boston: Little, Brown, 1996.

————. *Stokes Beginner's Guide to Birds: Western Region.* Boston: Little, Brown, 1996.

————. *Stokes Bird Feeder Book.* Boston: Little, Brown, 1987.

————. *Stokes Bird Gardening Book.* Boston: Little, Brown, 1998.

————. *Stokes Birdhouse Book.* Boston: Little, Brown, 1990.

————. *Stokes Field Guide to Birds: Eastern Region.* Boston: Little, Brown, 1996.

————. *Stokes Field Guide to Birds: Western Region.* Boston: Little, Brown, 1996.

————. *Stokes Guide to Bird Behavior, Volume II.* Boston: Little, Brown, 1983.

————. *Stokes Guide to Bird Behavior, Volume III.* Boston: Little, Brown, 1989.

————. *Stokes Hummingbird Book.* Boston: Little, Brown, 1989.

————. *Stokes Oriole Book.* Boston: Little, Brown, 2000.

————. *Stokes Wildflower Book: East of the Rockies.* Boston: Little, Brown, 1992.

————. *Stokes Wildflower Book: From the Rockies West.* Boston: Little, Brown, 1993.

MAGAZINES

Birder's World
P.O. Box 1612
Waukesha, WI 53187–1612
1-800-533-6644
http://www.birdersworld.com

Clifford's™ puppy days

THE LITTLE FLOWER SEED

by Sarah Fisch

Illustrated by Bob Roper

ISBN-13: 978-0-439-90899-3
ISBN-10: 0-439-90899-X

12 11 10 9 8 7 6   17 18 19 20/0

Designed by Michael Massen
Printed in the U.S.A.   40
First printing, March 2007

SCHOLASTIC INC.

| New York | Toronto | London | Auckland | Sydney |
| Mexico City | New Delhi | Hong Kong | Buenos Aires |

"Spring is in the air, Clifford!"
Emily Elizabeth said. "Can you feel it?"

Clifford wagged his tail. It was true!

"Early spring is the best time to plant a new garden," said Mrs. Howard.

"The courtyard will look pretty when our garden starts to bloom," Emily Elizabeth said.

"We'll have lots of vegetables and flowers in the garden, Clifford," Emily Elizabeth said. "Even some carrots for Daffodil!"

CAB

SWEET PEA

CARROT

TOMATO

EEDS

SE

SEEDS

SEEDS

Clifford looked and smelled, but he didn't
see any carrots or flowers!

Emily Elizabeth and her mother worked
and worked.

They dug holes in the dirt.

What fun! Clifford thought.

Then Emily Elizabeth dropped

something tiny into each hole.

Mrs. Howard covered each hole with dirt.

What's going on? Clifford wondered.

"All the seeds are planted!"
Emily Elizabeth shouted.

"Good work!" said Mrs. Howard.
"Let's go fill the watering can and
water our new garden."

Now it's my turn to dig! Clifford thought.

He dug and dug. *I'm helping, too!* he
thought.

"NO, NO, Clifford!" Emily Elizabeth shouted.

"Stop digging up the seeds!"

Clifford was so confused.

He didn't know what he did wrong!

"Seeds have to stay in the ground to become trees and flowers!" explained Emily Elizabeth.

This sounded strange to the tiny red puppy.

It rained the next day.

"Rain is good for gardens!" Daffodil
told Clifford.

"Why?" Clifford asked.

"Seeds need water to help them grow," Daffodil said.

In a few days, Clifford saw something wonderful!

The little flower seed had grown into
a tiny plant!

Soon all the seeds grew into tiny green
plants.

Clifford thought they were beautiful.

Emily Elizabeth watered the garden every day.

And every day, the weather got warmer and warmer.

The plants grew and grew!

The sunflower was Clifford's favorite.

When summer came, the puppy loved to

stay cool in its shade.

"Isn't it wonderful?" Mr. Sidarsky said.

"And the seeds are delicious!"

"You are a good gardener, Clifford,"
Daffodil said.

"This is the best carrot I've ever eaten!"

"Emily Elizabeth, you should be very proud," said Mr. Howard. "You grew a whole garden from little seeds!"

SUNFLOWER
SEEDS

Clifford barked happily. The sunflower was growing, and so was he. Who knew how big they'd both get?

Do You Remember?

Circle the right answer.

1. What did Emily Elizabeth tell Clifford to stop doing?
   - a. Barking at a cat
   - b. Chewing her shoe
   - c. Digging in the garden

2. Which is Daffodil's favorite?
   - a. Carrots
   - b. Sunflowers
   - c. Peas

Which happened first?

Which happened next?

Which happened last?

Write a 1, 2, or 3 in the space after each sentence.

It rained on the new garden. _____

Emily Elizabeth and Mrs. Howard planted seeds. _____

The sunflower grew taller than Clifford. _____

Answers

The sunflower grew taller than Clifford. (3)

Emily Elizabeth and Mrs. Howard planted seeds. (1)

It rained on the new garden. (2)

2. a

1. c